CHOOSING LIFE

CHOOSING LIFE

ONE MAN'S JOURNEY
THROUGH ALCOHOLISM AND DEPRESSION
TO WELLNESS AND SELF-DISCOVERY

a memoir by

Blue Andrews

LUMINARE PRESS
WWW.LUMINAREPRESS.COM

Luminare Press
442 Charnelton St.
Eugene, OR 97401
www.luminarepress.com

LCCN: 2022909712
ISBN: 978-1-64388-003-7

For my Grandma Mollie, who always wondered why I wasn't writing more.

Table of Contents

Preface

I wrote this book for me, to help in my recovery and growth, and for the challenge of completing a book I could be satisfied with.

I published this book for someone like me, or someone who cares about someone like me.

Diseases and deaths of despair are on the rise. Death by suicide, death from fatty liver or cirrhosis, depression, alcohol abuse—all on the rise. A large percentage of the victims, and in some cases the highest percentage, are middle-aged men.

And we aren't talking about it. At least we aren't talking about it enough.

My story, and stories like mine, are not new. We as a society have been dealing with these issues for decades. Maybe this is why it isn't more visible. Like poverty or homelessness, we are tired of hearing about it.

It also could be the case that men just aren't good at talking about their problems. Or society has trained us that we aren't supposed to talk about our problems, especially those squishy emotional and spiritual problems.

Or maybe it's because there isn't a simple solution. Life is complex. People are complex. A magic pill won't solve a person's life problems.

Whatever the reason, it seems as if we don't want to confront this issue head-on.

I didn't write this memoir because I think I have all the answers. I do believe I have one part of the solution, though. Sharing. My hope is that by sharing what went on in my life, all the ugly details, others will be more comfortable opening up about their lives. Once we get a problem out in the open, we have a better chance of solving it.

I also believe that most people don't really understand depression or alcoholism. Emotional struggles in general. That's because they are not easily describable. As is the case with physical health issues, there are no test results that can give us specifics about our emotional state in commonly understood terms. We can't give some blood, run it through the centrifuge, then get a piece of data to work with.

"Well, Mr. Andrews, it looks like your depressive proteins are at 101. You have stage three depression. Here is your protocol to reduce the depression." Then you go home and tell your family that you need to remove bacon from your diet and paint four hours a week for thirteen weeks.

That doesn't exist today.

Part of what I hope to share with this book is what it's like to feel depressed and then have Depression. What my type of alcoholism felt like. Either to connect with those who feel like me or help supporters understand what their loved ones may be experiencing.

In the end, I just want to raise my hand. Yes, I've had these problems. Yes, I know what it feels like. And, yes, there is a way out.

PART 1
DOWN

CHAPTER 1

LOSS

I arrived for my junior year of high school in Kirkland, Washington, lost and scared but mostly furious. I was dragged from my hometown of Roseburg, Oregon, following a year of success both on the field and in the classroom. Roseburg was an idyllic setting in which to grow up. It was a small logging town in the scenic Umpqua Valley of southern Oregon. Everyone knew everyone. Kids could ride their bikes anywhere in town any time of the day. Kirkland was a middle- to upper-middle-class suburb on the shores of Lake Washington, just across the lake from Seattle.

The week before I left, my picture was in the Roseburg newspaper as one of the top returning players on the football team. I was supposed to be sports editor for the *Orange R*, the high school newspaper. I had just finished an amazing sophomore year and finally felt like I was cool, which was all that had mattered to me since seventh grade. I knew nobody at Juanita High School. I knew nothing about Kirkland. I didn't care because it didn't matter. It was never going to be like Roseburg.

With my mom leaving my dad for good, the picture-perfect life I'd been living was yanked right out from underneath me. I hated my mom for moving us. I told her she stole all my confidence.

My parents had been fighting off and on for years. They probably never should have gotten married in the first place. My mom was only nineteen when my eighteen-year-old dad got her pregnant. Living in an even smaller town than Roseburg, in a much more conservative time, with my mom's parents so prominent, they did what they were told was "the right thing." They had me. I often thought not having me and not getting married would actually have been the right thing to do.

On the first day of school at Juanita, Scott Hardie saved me. He also played football and welcomed me a little bit before school started, saying "Hi" during late August practices. As friendly a guy as I had ever seen. Unbeknownst to the two of us at the time, we had English class together. Just as that period began, he grabbed his friends, including a few cute girls, and brought them over to sit next to me. It was so Scott. He didn't just invite me over to sit next to his crew. He made a huge scene by picking up desks and chairs, waving people over, and making sure that I, and everyone else, knew that he was coming to me. He made me feel important and wanted.

The following week he invited me to a party in his neighborhood. I couldn't believe it. I felt so lucky. My mom was thrilled I was making friends.

He gave me an address and general directions, but I couldn't find the place. It was in a subdivision with winding roads and street numbers that didn't make much sense. I had only been driving for about two months at that point. This was 1985, years before cell phones and ubiquitous GPS, so I just kept driving, turning, and searching for anything that might signal "house party." At one point, I got so far into the

Kingsgate neighborhood that I didn't even know if I could make it out. But I did, then found my bearings, and drove home. I walked into our apartment with tears in my eyes. My mom gave me a hug.

Not too long after that, the phone rang. It was Scott. I told him I couldn't find the place. He responded that he understood, admitting that his neighborhood was impossible to navigate, and offered to come over and pick me up. He arrived in what felt like two minutes. I later learned that Scott did everything at full speed.

I made it to the party. There were three guys there. That was it. It was pretty quiet. I would show them. I drank hard and fast. Spent a lot of time hovering over the toilet. What a start at my new school.

***

I started spending lots of time over at the Hardie house. Dinners. Sleepovers. Homework. The first time I spent the night at his house, we were up until four in the morning talking about all of those random things sixteen-year-old boys talk about. By the time the holiday season rolled around, the entire Hardie family had welcomed me. They gave me the nicest Christmas present I'd ever received up until that point, a Levi's jean jacket with faux sheepskin lining.

***

Later that school year, my friend group expanded when Todd took me in. Todd may have been the most popular kid in the junior class, if not the whole school, and I idolized him. Blond hair, blue eyes, and a dimpled smile that caused moms to stutter. Before Matthew McConoughey, there was Todd.

Todd was a hand-clapper, a motivator who rallied those around him. He was the guy in the middle of the players' circle leading the chant before the game. Scott was my support. Todd became my booster fuel, lifting my spirits.

Todd took me to a few big parties, helped grow my social circle. He also showed me that the fun actually began when we ventured off looking for the party. On many Friday or Saturday nights, Todd didn't know exactly whose party we were going to or where exactly the party was. He just had "heard" about a party. My first instinct was fear. *What if we didn't find the party?* I wondered how Todd could be so bold to think that he could just search this big ol' town and find the party he was looking for? He'd just keep smiling and laughing.

When we were on the field or the court, it seemed he had no problem with pressure or future trippin'. Just looked like he was having fun. I played as if it were life or death. For him, it was always "no worries, just relax." He began to embody everything excellent about Juanita. Winning. Free spirit. Just having fun.

He was one of the few other boys who were three-sport athletes in the class, so we became better and better friends throughout the school year. As summer rolled around, we were hanging out quite a bit. Hitting parties in his convert-ible '60s MG. Chasing girls. Baseball games. Pick-up hoops. Off-season football drills.

About midsummer, Todd wasn't showing up for prac-tices. I found out he went to Australia with a baseball team that included a bunch of Juanita ballplayers. I felt jealous. Another reminder that I still was not "in" at Juanita. Then I remembered, we didn't have the money for that sort of thing anyway. I still didn't know how there was enough money for my glove and cleats. *How do all of these people have enough money to go to Australia to play baseball?*

When Todd returned, he brought back a song that he had discovered. "Spirit in the Sky," by Norman Greenbaum. That cassette sounded so good blaring out of the deck in his MG.

We ended the summer prepping for our senior year. Football practice started—time to defend our back-to-back state championships. Six seniors were selected as co-captains, including both Todd and me.

The first Friday of my senior year in high school, during the afternoon before the first football game of the year, a couple of Todd's closest buddies invited me to hang out with them. Here I was, the new kid, at Art's apartment with two of the cool kids, waiting for Todd to arrive.

Art seemed a little uncomfortable in his apartment, maybe embarrassed because it wasn't a real house. That place was being remodeled. Seemed completely fine to me. My apartment was in the complex right next door, and its 800 square feet of living space was about as much as I'd ever known, even though it was smaller than his. Besides, what could be wrong? I was hanging out with these guys.

We were joking about where we would party after beating whoever we were scheduled to play that night when the phone rang. I assumed it would be Todd letting us know he was on his way, but he had to run home because he had forgotten something. Todd was always late, carrying his own drum.

Art picked up the phone.

"What?" he said. Then he mouthed, "Suzie," to us. My ears perked up. I couldn't hear what she was saying exactly, but I could hear her screaming, crying voice all the way from the other side of the room.

"Todd's what?" Art asked. "What!?" he asked again. Then he just hung up the phone, hands shaking, face red.

"Todd died," Art stammered.

Silence. Disbelief. I could not make sense of what I had just heard. We all just looked at each other. What? and Huh? were all that our seventeen-year-old faces could express.

"How?" we finally asked.

"Something at his job."

"What do we do?" we eventually said.

"We should head down there," we agreed.

I had no answer. I still didn't feel like I belonged there, and I wasn't about to contribute an idea. We hopped in John's truck, a classic, red Ford F-150, and didn't say a word during the few-minute drive to the accident. It felt like it took forever. I wished it would have taken longer.

The details of the freak incident are blurry. Todd had been working a part-time job. An old structure, electricity, a metal ladder, and gravity were involved. He was killed instantly.

I couldn't believe Todd was dead. There was just no way. He was invincible.

We slowly pulled up to the scene and parked. I sat there for a bit before getting out of the truck. Multiple first responders were there, lights still rotating. People were milling about. Other Juanita Rebels started rolling in with their hands over their mouths, arms around each other's shoulders. Crying faces buried in chests.

I was taking the entire scene in by myself, again alone. Those people were Todd's real friends. They knew him much longer than I had. I began to shift away from everyone, trying to understand what was going on, feeling the need to be alone to process what was happening.

Since I couldn't see a dead Todd, I could still convince myself there must not be a dead Todd.

The EMTs seemed to be surrounded in one particular spot, but too many people were between them and me. I moved across the street, staggering, trying to get away from the crowd. Eventually, I found an open view. There it was. A black tarp covering a body up to the forehead, beautiful blond hair the only part of Todd I could see.

I couldn't breathe. My hands hit my knees, and I started bawling. Uncontrollably. Loud. Wailing. All by myself. I tried to stand but had to bend back over. I tried to move, but my feet didn't want me to leave that view. I just kept staring at that mop of hair, imprinting an image of death into my brain.

The following week, I mustered up the courage to write about Todd's death in our school newspaper. Since I was one of the editors, I was able to write two pieces. One was a news piece, doing my best to be an objective reporter describing the tragedy. The other was a lifestyle piece, written with fondness and jest, hoping to help my classmates deal with our loss.

We listened to "Spirit in the Sky" a lot that fall.

With Todd's death staring at me every day at school, my mom's breast cancer cloaked my mind at home.

During the winter of my junior year in high school, that first year at my new school, my mom was diagnosed with breast cancer. The diagnosis arrived not too long after I felt like I was starting to fit in, about six months after moving, around the time I started hanging with Todd. Not truly understanding its severity, I was relatively unfazed by the revelation when she shared the news. Mom started going to chemo, and I kept going to school and practice. She had such a positive mindset around me. I was sure cancer wasn't going to beat her. She would overcome this. It seemed to never be a big deal for her, and there wasn't anyone else around to make a big deal of it, so it wasn't a big deal for me. We never talked about the fact that she could die.

She was in and out of treatment, then in remission for a bit, but the cancer was back and growing by summer. They tried more intense treatments but were unsuccessful. My mom's cancer wasn't going away.

By this time, late summer, when things were really rolling for me socially and athletically, she made the decision to move down to Portland to be with her sister. Kay had some experience in the burgeoning world of homeopathy and naturopathy, using herbs and alternative medicines instead of drugs for healing. Since there seemed to be no traditional solutions, my mom decided to continue the fight with the help of my aunt's network of healers.

There weren't many conversations about this. In a good Christian home, parents command and children obey. I learned to just accept my mom's decisions and didn't protest when she moved three hours away to live in Portland with Aunt Kay.

I was by myself. My brother, still in junior high, was there. My Uncle Tom stopped in periodically to check on us and spend the night. But, basically, at seventeen, I was taking care of myself.

Without much structure and zero guidance at home, I began to zone out. A few games into the football season, I wasn't even starting anymore, so I quietly relinquished my captain role. I was skipping assignments in class, leading to a two-point-something GPA that semester, including an F in English.

My thoughts meandered all over during those autumn months alone in that little apartment. School, sports, friends. Last year, next year. Confusion, frustration, isolation. Of course, my thinking constantly kept coming back to my mom.

I wondered about my mother's teenage years. *Was she as distraught as me when her life changed? Where was her mom while she was struggling?*

My mom was a freshman at Gonzaga University when she became pregnant with me. She came from a stable home in the little town of Milton-Freewater in northeast Oregon, just below the Blue Mountains. They were not rich in big city terms, but they were well-off. My grandpa had his own law practice by day and was a community leader the rest of the time. As part of a small group of men who formally brought the towns of Milton and Freewater together, he drafted the legal documents and did much of the negotiating between the two towns. He volunteered with the Rotary Club among other organizations. Many times he traded his services for a chicken or a box of produce, whatever the family could give. My grandma supported him and was active in the community herself.

My mom was a Pea Princess in the annual Milton-Freewater Pea Festival. She rode horses, played sports and was active in school. Above all, she was the eldest Monahan kid in town. An important role, one she tried to uphold.

Underneath this image, she struggled emotionally. As a teenager, anxiety got the best of her, causing most of her hair to fall out. She resorted to wearing wigs for a while. Even though she had a contagious smile, I wondered what was going on behind the grin when I looked at photographs of her youth.

I had acquired a fake ID the fall prior and had figured out a couple of clever ways of obtaining alcohol. One of my favorites was acting as the supportive father. I would cut class—because, of course, the guy in the fake ID, Tom Hanover, was no longer in high school—and buy beer or wine coolers along with diapers and food. The other way to get alcohol was to get dropped off about a half-mile from a mini-mart in the rain. That way, I looked the part of a person who honestly had no driver's license, just an ID card, which was really nothing more than a laminated piece of paper with my picture on it and a date from more than twenty-one years ago.

On nights when my uncle wasn't over, I would stay up late having a drink or two. Never getting totally wasted, just breaking the rules. On nights when my uncle was over, we would stay up late having meandering discussions that could easily touch on math, girls, sports, abortion, and God over the course of an hour or two. Those were post-midnight bedtimes also.

I was an emotional kid with super highs and super lows. I made the all-star team and it was the greatest day in the history of the world. I struck out and I was the worst baseball player ever. My mom shrugged at the good stuff like it was supposed to happen. Laughed at the bad, like it was nothing. All that was outside me didn't mean anything to her anyway. She loved me no matter what. She was there no matter what. Except now.

My mom managed that fine line of wanting to participate in every aspect of my life while giving me room to grow up on my own. Even though we didn't have any money, she always provided new gear for my sports. I was always able to make it to events and friends' houses and games. I rode my bike to practices, but she never missed any of my scheduled events, from games to spelling bees to plays. I could always look up into the crowd and find her, alone and radiant. I couldn't miss her.

Our home was where my friends would hang out or play, even though we didn't have much in the way of toys or food. My mom's attitude made up for the lack of material stuff. Her huge smile and contagious laugh. Her always-ready hugs and ever-on jokes. She could make fun of us yet make us feel like we were a part of the joke, not the joke itself. She loved every one of my friends, and they knew it.

All of that was now gone. My mom's presence, just her presence, comforted me. Even that was taken from me.

Football season ended and basketball season started. I was ready for a new start. With Todd gone, I was voted co-captain, the only senior in the starting lineup. After a preseason game in Kent, about an hour south of Kirkland, my coach came over to me in the locker room. He sat down next to me and let me know I wouldn't be taking the team bus home. He said my aunt and uncle were there with my brother, and we would be heading down to Portland. My teammates watched in silence as the news was delivered. I knew what this meant. Maybe they did too.

Mom's time was coming to an end.

I got out of the locker room and walked down the hallway to meet my family. We hugged, but no tears were shed. We quietly made our way to their gray VW Vanagon.

About an hour south of Kent in the small town of Chehalis, we saw a big ol' neon sign, "The Rib Eye." Dinner time. I was starving. The Monahans could always eat. We looked over the huge menu and started suggesting appetizers that sounded good. The list kept growing, so my uncle just ordered every one of them. Every single one. It was awesome. We laughed. Nearly ate them all. Plus dinner. And a couple of desserts. Anything to provide a distraction and prolong our arrival.

I got ready to see my mom in the morning, having no idea what I was getting into. I hadn't seen her in about three months. The house was made of dark wood, surrounded by tall evergreens. I walked in and saw adults milling about.

There was a couch next to the front window. Hushed murmurs filled in from different corners of different rooms. Glances in my direction. Mom was in one of the bedrooms. At some point, I was told I could go in and see her.

She was lying down, looking groggy. A few scraps of hair had grown back. I couldn't tell if she was asleep, drugged up or what. She didn't look or feel like my mom. I walked over to the other side of the bed and said, "Hi, Mom."

I think she reached out for me, or maybe I reached out for her, but we touched, very gently. Then all I heard was a loud scream. "Owwww!!! It hurts so bad! I'm in so much pain," she said. Then, more quietly, "It hurts so bad. Just hurts so bad."

I freaked out. *I hurt my mother! I just tortured my mom!* I ran out of the room and sat on the couch. I looked at all of the adults but didn't verbalize my confusion and fear. I faded inside myself. An adult came over and told me it wasn't my fault. Women started patting me, my hand, my shoulder, my head.

As I was sleeping in my hotel room that night, Grandpa came in and turned on the lights. "She passed," is all he said before walking out of the room. I smiled when he told me that. *Huh? What was that all about?* I put my clothes on and got in one of the cars. I wasn't crying. Just silent.

What now?

We went back to the house. I was told it was my turn to go see her. Not much had changed in that room. She was in the same place, in the same position. Just colder. I gently put my hand on her shoulder, softly touched her hand, laid my hand on her forehead for just a bit. I didn't say a word; then, suddenly, as if I wasn't doing it right, I just left the room.

As the sun rose higher in the sky, I thought: *I should be hurting. I should be in pain. I should be feeling something terrible.* I wasn't. I was just there. Eventually, I got up off the couch without saying a word, headed out the door, and decided to start sprinting up and down the hill, wanting to force pain into my body. I wanted my legs to burn. I wanted to throw up. Feel the pain that my mom had gone through. Feel the pain that you're supposed to feel when your mom dies. Feel something, anything, bad. I still hadn't cried like I did with Todd. But no matter how hard I ran, I couldn't ever get there. After working up a sweat, I gave up. *This is dumb. How am I supposed to feel? How did other people feel when their mom died? Would someone just tell me what I was supposed to be doing? How I should be feeling.*

What was I supposed to do now?

That was December 13, 1986. I was seventeen. Over the next couple of weeks, a few things happened during the holiday break from school. I don't remember much, certainly not the actual sequence of events, but I know they happened.

There was a memorial for my mom in Kirkland. Someone organized it. Someone, or maybe a few people, said something. *Where did all of these people come from? How did my mom have this many friends? How did she meet them?* I didn't know many adults there, and it made me feel as if I hadn't been paying attention. *Where have I been?*

My basketball coach had the entire team come to the service. I smiled when I saw them in the back row, all in a line. These unknown people were there for my mom; they were there for me. I could hang on to them.

There was also a memorial for my mom in Roseburg. Someone organized it. Someone, or maybe a few people, said something. There were even more people at this service. I am not sure what was said, but I did a lot of chatting that day.

After the memorial services were held, a time that seemed to drag on forever, the adults talked about where my brother and I should live. The Hardies offered to take me in, as did the Crossfields, my mom's best friends in Roseburg. Other families stepped in, from all over it seemed, offering a place I could call home.

I wanted to stay in Juanita. I loved it up there. The world was so much bigger in Kirkland than in Roseburg. But I didn't get my first, or even second, choice because my dad demanded that I live with him. I especially didn't want to live with my dad.

My dad was worthless to me. While we were growing up, he took off so many times. When he was around, most of the time it felt like he was angry at the world. I wanted no part of that attitude. However, one thing he said stuck with me.

When I was about nine and my brother six, my mom was babysitting this boy who was somewhere in age between us. He looked up to me and did whatever I was interested in. Of course, my little brother did not. One day the two of them got in a fight, and I took the side of the friend. My dad got home and drilled into me that you always stick up for your brother. No matter what. So when my brother, who didn't have such a good time in Kirkland, said he wanted to go back to Roseburg, I agreed. It wasn't as if I really had a choice. As all of the adults in my life reminded me, my dad was in charge.

I had a going-away party at the apartment in Kirkland, which started late afternoon and finished early morning. I got drunk as about ten or twenty friends came over to say goodbye. Even after all of them had left, I didn't cry.

After Christmas break, sixteen months after leaving, I walked back into Roseburg High School as if nothing had changed. I made it through school, playing basketball and baseball, worked on the school newspaper, took my honors classes, and graduated. That summer, my dad thought he did me a favor by getting me a job at the local cemetery digging and maintaining gravesites. All summer long, I stared at headstones, looking at their dates, wondering.

———

I know that she loved being a mom, but I also believed I should have never been born. If one of my children were in the same situation as my parents, I would strongly suggest not giving birth. I absolutely changed the course of my mom's life. Not purposely. She made a decision. Her support network made a decision. My dad was who he was. But, if she hadn't gotten pregnant with me at age nineteen, her life would have been very different. Maybe she wouldn't have been tortured by my dad and her mom during the entirety of her adult life. Maybe she could have been her own person, discovered her own life. Maybe cancer never would have prevailed if the stressors hadn't broken down her immune system. What if?

———

I graduated from Roseburg and had no idea what I wanted to do when I grew up. I just knew I was supposed to go to college.

Before my mom died, I had an opportunity to attend the Air Force Academy. However, after having lunch with officers and other candidates at McChord Air Force Base, I decided I didn't want to serve in the military. I submitted the lengthy application for the journalism program at Northwestern University, went to the Westin Hotel in Seattle for an interview, but didn't communicate with them after that.

Back in Roseburg, my dad wondered why the community college in Roseburg wasn't good enough for me. The University of Oregon and the University of Washington each had one-page applications. So easy. About all I could handle. I was so, so tired. No essays or interviews required. I haphazardly filled out both applications. I got accepted to both. Longing to be back in Seattle, I chose the UW.

College was a relatively solid time for me. I joined a fraternity of over one hundred guys and lived there for four years. I went back to Roseburg during my first two summers and worked at the plywood mill pulling dry belt. The final summer I worked for a few different companies moving and installing school and office furniture.

During the spring of 1991, at age twenty-one, I was set to get my bachelor's degree in economics. Not knowing anything about getting a real job, I worked through the UW's career placement center and applied for dozens of jobs. I got interviews with a few and was even flown down to San Francisco for second interviews with one. Eventually, I took a job as a sales rep with Playtex Family Products selling tampons in Orange County, California. The company marketed baby products, rubber gloves, and a few lines of hair care products, but 35% of its revenue came from the feminine hygiene section. I was a tampon salesman.

Between my name and my job, I always had something to talk about.

I didn't know a thing about Southern California, but, again, Scott saved me. A couple of college buddies lived in an ideal location for my job. One was a longtime family friend, the other a football teammate. After a couple of phone calls, I was invited to squeeze in with them in their two-bedroom apartment a few minutes from Newport Beach. They were frat guys as well, so tight quarters were nothing new to them, either.

Quickly, I was promoted twice and was making more money than I could have imagined while growing up in Roseburg. At twenty-two, I managed a million-dollar account and trained new salespeople, some of whom were twice my age.

I spent a couple of rock-star weekends partying in Hollywood with a friend from Roseburg who lived up in L.A. proper. Running up a $300 tab on pitchers of margaritas at an outdoor cantina across from the beach in Santa Monica. Pool parties with models. Slipping through an unmarked door into a room full of The Beautiful People, picking up rounds of whatever they wanted. What an adventure for a small-town hick.

I had an incredible year in Orange County, exploring beaches and bars. Loved wearing shorts on Thanksgiving Day. As fun as all of that was, the job didn't feel like it led to a career that would keep me interested. Was I really going to be challenged and captivated by this industry, by baby bottles and hair conditioner, for forty years? I wanted to get into software. My uncle was a programmer, and it just seemed like such an exciting thing to be a part of, full of youth and ambition. After a little more than a year, I dropped everything and moved back to Kirkland, just a few miles down State Route 202 from the worldwide headquarters of Microsoft.

Scott's parents had a rental house a few blocks from where he grew up. I moved in with him and one of my best friends from the fraternity at the UW. A fresh start filled with youthful excitement.

I submitted résumé after résumé to any computer-related company in the Seattle area. After about two months of trying and dozens of no responses, a friend from both high school and the fraternity let me know about an opening at the little software company he was working for. They were looking for some temp help through the holiday season. I lucked out and got the job, then busted my butt, taking upwards of one hundred customer service and inside sales calls a day. A few weeks later, after the Christmas rush, I interviewed for and was offered a full-time job as a channel sales rep.

Scott had his architecture degree from Cal Poly and immediately found a job with a firm in Seattle. He was so smart and an amazing artist. It seemed like the perfect career for him, and I was so pumped he landed a job in that field right out of college.

We were freewheeling! Ideal jobs. Living together in Kirkland. *How cool is this!?*

Just months into our dream careers, Scott told me he was crapping and pissing blood. *What!? What the hell is going on? He's probably just exaggerating. Blood?*

A few days later, Scott told me that he couldn't keep food down. A few days after that, he told me he couldn't eat enough, that he was never full. I asked him about the blood. "Yep," he said. "That's still going on too."

Scott was twenty-two years old and as fit a guy as I'd ever been around. Even after his college football days ended, he kept up intense workouts. He ate the cleanest diet of anyone I knew, including drinking way less than anyone I knew. Yet here Scott was talking about bowel, stomach, and digestive problems!? Crazy.

After a few weeks of this, he went to the doctor. He was diagnosed with leiomyosarcoma, a type of cancer that attacks the smooth muscles that line many digestive organs. I could not process it. It made no sense. Didn't think it was real. *It can't be that bad. It must be a misdiagnosis.*

Scott went after that cancer like he did everything in life—110% and smiling. He started with traditional treatments. His hair thinned until one day he walked in the front door bald, just like his idol Michael Jordan. Conventional treatments weren't working, so he researched and tried alternative routes. My favorite was shark cartilage, a cutting-edge alternative "treatment." But that wasn't working either.

It was only a matter of time.

Scott had been dating an incredible woman who stuck with him through every step of his struggle with cancer. Scott was in love and was so thankful for her. He wanted to propose, knowing full well he wasn't going to make it to the altar. Such a Scott gesture. It was also his way of looking at life. Just a glimmer of hope was all he needed.

I was honored that he asked me to cook the meal that they would have before the proposal. I was also heartbroken. Scott didn't have the strength to go out to eat. He didn't have the strength to cook a decent meal on his own. Yet, he wanted to give. Somehow, in some way, he was going to give. Show his love. I made a green salad and a raspberry vinaigrette dressing, baked salmon with a fruit sauce, steamed vegetables, and rice. Only the healthiest for Scott, even at this stage. I gave him directions on when and how to reheat it before the big proposal. It was the best afternoon. Just Scott and me. Our friendship felt whole again.

I left him alone, went out to my car, drove around the corner and sobbed until my shoulders hurt.

I walked into Scott's hospital room and my knees buckled. He was bald. I had almost gotten used to that. What I couldn't handle were all the tubes. Up his nose. In his arms and wrists.

Under his gown into some part of his core. Connected to bags of clear liquid and the beeping machines.

This was it. Scott was dying. *How could this possibly be? In what universe does this make sense? How does my strength become so weak? So frail? So helpless?* This guy who was so kind and caring, intelligent and thoughtful, strong and hard-working. He was my age, and I was so young. None of it, not even the slightest flicker, was making any sense.

Scott's was my first eulogy.

I couldn't believe the Hardies asked me to do it. He had so many great friends, so many more friends with richer and longer histories. I am not sure why or how I said yes, but I am so grateful I did.

I felt the audience laugh, felt them cry. I told the few stories that I figured would capture the Scott I knew. I hoped he knew, and the audience knew, and his family knew, how much I loved him. That's all I wanted. And a little relief from the trauma.

After I was done, I went back to my seat next to Mike, my Orange County roommate, now more family than friend. As people were standing to leave, Bette Midler's "Wind Beneath My Wings" came on. Scott was my hero. He saved me at least three times. He exemplified the best in people. I couldn't stop crying. I didn't want to get up. I just wanted to soak that song in. But I took my place in line and carried my tears out to the lobby. Taking a seat in what I thought was a hidden corner, I could barely talk. I was hunched over, crying and shaking. "Well done" and "What a beautiful speech," they all said.

I could barely see who they were through the tears.

Scott's mom, Nancy, became a second mom to me, my Kirkland Mom. Though I never got to tell her that.

"Jeff," she would call me. "Nance," I would respond. Jeffrey is my first name. Blue is my middle, the only one most people know. Having her call me Jeff meant she really knew me and made it something special. Having a nickname for her just felt a little irreverent, something I could have never pulled off with my real mom. More importantly, a thing just between us. She would never be my real mom, but she deserved something more than what everyone else called her.

Nancy was a stand-in Mom to many of the boys in Scott's circle. She just had that "mom" thing. A disciplinarian, but a lighthearted one. She'd get on you when you screwed up but always had a warm smile once the brain of a teenage boy recognized that something wrong had taken place. She joked with us as if we were friends, then told us to clean up after ourselves. And she hugged. A real mom hug. The everything-is-going-to-be-OK hug.

About six years after Scott's death, Nancy was diagnosed with cancer also. Breast, just like my real mom. She died rather suddenly after the diagnosis. After her immune system had broken down to such a great degree, necrotizing fasciitis, the skin-eating disease, took over. I was able to say goodbye one last time during her final few hours, then was able to give an angel blessing just after she passed.

My brand-new wife, Sandy, and I had a trip to Argentina planned. We were to leave just days after Nance died. With Sandy's dad's strong recommendation, we postponed our Argentina trip. It was one of the best recommendations I ever listened to. I was able to participate in Nancy's service, although I didn't have to come up with any of my own material this time. Just read someone else's. I spent many hours at the Hardies' in those few days after Nancy died. I formed strong bonds with many of Nancy's other "kids" and felt part of an extended family in that house over those few days. I hadn't felt part of a big family before. After my mom died, I became very close with her parents and siblings. My brother and I grew closer, but we weren't best friends yet. Neither my aunt nor uncle were married at the time. No cousins yet on that side of the family. I was not close with my dad, so relationships with his family were barely existent. Just a handful of people made up what I would consider family.

The people surrounding the Hardies looked like family. These people cared about each other. Their lives were intertwined. I wondered if this was what extra aunts and uncles and cousins would feel like.

When Nance died, I lived over on the other side of the lake, in the city. I found the girl beyond my dreams. I had an extraordinary job that took me all over the country, to cities I'd never visited. I was listening to grunge music, drinking these newfangled drinks called lattes from Starbucks, and celebrating being part of the dot-com scene.

But I couldn't find my way back to the other side of Lake Washington, to Kirkland. I could see it from Seattle, but I could not physically make it there. I was afraid to step foot in my old stomping grounds. So, while I lived the life of a 1990s Seattle twenty-something, memories of Kirkland haunted me. The anguish of watching people die just engulfed me, like fog rolling across the water. I couldn't address the grief, so I began drowning in it.

CHAPTER 2

Dad

When I was in grade school, my dad had a crappy job. Working at a national retail jewelry store chain, Zales or some-such, meant working weekends, evenings, and holidays. Every day his feet and back hurt, or he had a headache, or he was "sick and tired" of dealing with "idiot" customers. Although, as I would realize later in life, my dad thought everyone was an asshole, a jerk, or a loser. Everyone. My friends' parents. Neighbors. Other people who worked downtown.

My mom would try to have dinner ready for him when he got home. He wouldn't say much at the dinner table, hiding behind those glasses that would move from clear to gray to dark, depending on how much light was in the room. To me, they were mood glasses. The darker they got, the meaner he was.

"Eat what's there because you never know if there's going to be enough next time," was a favorite of my dad's.

After dinner, Dad would roll over to His Chair. No one else would ever dare to sit in that chair, though I would sneak into it sometimes when I knew he was at work, thinking, "I'm running the show now." He'd turn the TV on, light up a cigarette, and just sit there, not saying much of anything. Usually, most of the lights were off because too much light would worsen his headaches. My mom rushed into the kitchen, just over the counter from His Chair, and cleaned up, saving whatever she could for leftovers the next day. I loved the leftovers for breakfast and lunch, not that there was ever much choice of what I was going to eat.

Most nights after dinner, I would venture off to make up a game that involved a ball, outside if it was light out, back in my room otherwise. I loved playing catch, any kind of catch—footballs, baseballs, tennis balls, raw eggs—anything that could be thrown and caught. For hours at a time I would play, using the side of our house as my partner. Sometimes I would have a racket in my hand, sometimes a baseball mitt. Most of the time, it was just my hands. If I really wanted to hone my skills, I would step off the smooth cement of the carport onto the dry, bumpy dirt and grass lawn of our side yard, attempting to field unpredictable ground balls as they ricocheted off the uneven wall. I would set goals. Ten in a row. Twenty-five in a row. Fifty in a row. The goals would adjust up and down based on my skill level that day. I would get lost in the challenge, determined not to let the wall or the ground or my own weakness beat me. A ball and that wall were all I needed for much of my grade school years.

Every once in a while, I would gather up the nerve to tell Dad about my day. There were times I would have something good to share with him. "Well, whoop-de-doo, good for you," was the level of response I would get. Other times I would share something that was troubling me. "Yeah, well, life sucks, then you die," would be his response to that. Life sucks, then you die. Another favorite out of the old man.

If what I did was against his rules, he would take me over his knee and pound me.

There was a rickety old fence, all grayed out with splinters everywhere, between our backyard and one of our neighbors. One day a hardball slammed into it, causing a little break in one of the boards. I went up to the hole and peeked through, now able to see our neighbor's backyard. Curious whether I could get a better view, I found a hammer and made another hole. Then another. I could see a whole lot of the other backyard. *Excellent.*

Then I stopped. *Uh-oh. That's a lot of holes.* My mom noticed too. She told me I was in trouble, and Dad would punish me when he got home. I dreaded it all day long. I knew what was coming.

We went into my parents' room, and my dad sat on the end of the bed. He said, "This hurts me more than it hurts you." *Huh? Right.* I leaned over him, and he took that cheeseboard, about the size of his forearm, and beat me with it until I cried. Then I stood up, and my dad made me hug him. I hated that part. Why would I want to hug him after he did that to me?

"I'm doing this for your own good. I love you son," he said. That never made sense to me either.

On many occasions, including this broken fence incident, both my brother and I got in trouble. We would wait all day for our spankings. Unlike me, though, my brother refused to give my dad a hug after his initial beating. Or even the second or third. "Give me a hug," my dad would say. My brother would just shake his head. "You're going to get it again if you don't give me a hug," my dad would warn. And another beating came. Then another.

Sometimes I got to leave the room after my punishment was served, but the house wasn't big enough to hide my brother's crying and screaming, or my dad's voice getting louder and angrier. *Why don't you just hug him and get it over with? Please, just hug him!*

At least my brother would take a stab at some sort of defiance. I was too afraid, knowing full well that we would get destroyed if we ever really tried to fight back. While I hurt for my little brother, and felt ashamed I wouldn't stand by him, I was so amazed by the boldness of his little rebellion.

My paternal grandfather was an abusive drunk who hit his wife and kids. The other four boys, that is, but not my dad. Men, including his dad, were afraid of him even when he was a kid, or so his stories went. They had no money, less than the no money I grew up with, and the eight of them lived in various tiny houses, even a barn for a while. Sometimes no Christmas presents at all, sometimes a pair of socks if they were lucky. His childhood included literally watching a chicken run around with its head chopped off as his mom prepared Sunday supper. After it was cooked, at the dinner table, he scrambled to get every last scrap of that cooked bird. When I was young, I watched my dad eat all parts of the animal that no one else would touch. I knew he was telling the truth about the world he grew up in.

I never knew my dad's dad. He died before I was born. Alcoholism, they say. It could have been a liver disease since my dad and two of his brothers were struck with some variation of disorder in that organ. Regardless of the diagnosis, I could only imagine downing a bunch of booze couldn't have helped.

At the ripe age of nineteen, my dad, Steven Wayne Andrews, who had just graduated from high school and was dating my mom, a star of the town, found himself staring at her belly with me in there. Having decided to keep the kid and no longer feeling welcome in Milton-Freewater, my parents moved to New Mexico, a place my mom had never been. My dad had relatives and the slightest of job prospects, so away they went.

My first three years were in New Mexico, first in Farmington, where I was born, then in Roswell, where my brother was born. But both of my parents longed to be back in the Northwest, so we moved to Oregon. After a couple of years in the Portland area, we ended up in Roseburg, where I grew up.

My dad took off on us about ten times from that little house on NW Keasey Street. Just a night or two most of the time. Once there were rumors about an underage girl that lived down the road from us. Another time it was bad enough that my mom took my brother and me to Cannon Beach, on the Oregon Coast, for the summer. We stayed with her sister, my Aunt Kay. I knew something was troubling my mom but didn't truly understand what was happening. She cried frequently and started smoking cigarettes. As conservative as my mom was, and as far to the other end as my aunt was, I wouldn't have been surprised if she tried smoking weed too.

I don't recall ever asking about my dad. I just knew he didn't come with us. It was still a great summer.

My aunt's place wasn't too far from the ocean if you took a straight shot through overgrowth and forest. My brother and I began the summer by hacking a sizable pathway through sky-high blackberry bushes. That opened the door to an overgrowth forest. Massive fir and cedar trees created a canopy over the needle-covered ground below. Fallen logs fashioned fertile ground for ferns and mushrooms. Trolls and gnomes must have lived in there as well.

It was all ours. No one but us was ever in there. Well, except for our make-believe friends—Steve and Walkie. We pretended we were on dirt bikes, running as fast as we could up and down hills, jumping over logs, kicking off trees. We were thoroughly entertained pretending and creating in that playground nature created.

When the summer ended, the three of us went back to Roseburg. Mom giving Dad yet another chance.

My dad wasn't all bad. When his emotions were just right, my dad would get out of his La-Z-Boy, put the cigarettes and beer down, turn off the TV, and play catch with me. When my dad was like this, his good self, he was great. Charismatic and funny. Smart and active. I never expected it, but I sure did love Happy Dad when he came around.

In the fall of 1978, I was nine years old, and the Oakland Raiders had just come off their first Super Bowl victory. Kenny Stabler and Freddy Biletnikoff were the top pass-catching tandem in the NFL. After Sunday church, at halftime of the game—back then, there was only one football game on at a time, and only two to choose from the entire day—I grabbed the Nerf football. My dad became Stabler, the outlaw quarterback with matching beard and attitude. I was Biletnikoff, the long-haired, scruffy receiver.

Most of the time, while we were playing catch, he would be a commentator for the game.

"It's third and long. The Raiders have the ball deep in their own territory. Freddy Biletnikoff off to the right. Stabler behind center. Hut, hut, hike. He takes the snap and drops back. Biletnikoff goes deep up the sideline. He cuts across the field. A long pass from Stabler. Caught! Touchdown Raiders!!!" Our side yard really was one hundred yards long, I really did score a touchdown for the world champs, and my dad was there for it all.

My dad's arm wore out long before my legs or my enthusiasm. He had a bum shoulder and a couple of scars. One of them was an indentation right up near his shoulder socket. It looked like a football had slammed into his skin at two hundred miles per hour. When I asked if that was what happened, he paused, shook his head, and said, "Sure, you bet, son." The other scar was from a barbed-wire fence that he got tangled up in during a fight. With a cold look on his face, he told me that he didn't even feel it. "Not like the pain the other guy was feelin'."

During baseball season, we would play "hot toss" with baseballs and mitts. We would back up a fair distance, and I would start throwing the ball as hard as I could at my dad. He would throw it pretty dang hard right back at me. We would move closer and closer to each other, one step at a time, until we were just a few feet apart. But the velocity of our throws wouldn't change. Faster and faster until I became one with the ball, and I could handle any throw. We would go until one of us caught a BB in the wrong part of the mitt, smack in the palm. The glove would drop. Ow! That was the sign that told me I played as hard as I possibly could.

Other times we would play catch with an egg, just the opposite of hot toss. We would toss it softly, from just a few feet apart. Then we would take a step back, still the softest throw possible. We got so far apart that I became both nervous and exhilarated, knowing that any minute, with any throw, that egg could explode, yolk and shell splatting all over me. Eventually, the egg would break, and my dad would laugh.

Such a great laugh, full-bodied with a twinkle in his eye and softness flowing from his heart. A kid just like me.

My dad didn't like coming to my baseball games when I was young. He did make a few when I was in high school, but rather than sitting in the bleachers with my teammates' families and friends, he chose to take a lawn chair and plop it down just outside the right field foul pole. He sat all by himself in a Hawaiian shirt, fully unbuttoned if the sun was out, which also meant an iced-down cooler sitting on the ground next to him. I tried not to focus on it, but *what the hell, Dad?*

For my dad's birthday one year, my mom decided we would get pictures made. I couldn't believe it. We were not a big picture-taking family. The Monahans did not like looking at themselves in photographs, no matter how joyful the occasion or excellent the backdrop. My dad never seemed like he was in the mood for "capturing the moment." Besides, we didn't have any money for this. But here we were out at River Forks Park, where the North Umpqua River slammed into the South, forming the mighty Umpqua. A beautiful setting of water, hills, trees, and meadows. As far as I was concerned, though, the park and playground were the best part, with the fort and teepees, water fountain, and yards and yards of open grass to run around in. If we were going to do this silly picture thing, I conceded that this was a pretty great spot to do it.

At my mother's insistence, we cleaned up a bit, and my brother and I put on what might pass for our Sunday best. Toughskins and a button-down shirt. Total cost easily less than five dollars. Our hair was fine, just as it was, a couple of full heads that naturally flowed into strong '70s pop-rock star fashion. Think a young James Taylor or Glenn Frey.

Looking good and feeling weird, we bounced around various parts of the park, escorted by a professional photographer my mom knew through a friend of a friend. We climbed on the fort, staggered ourselves amongst the trees and took tough-guy poses near the swings. "Smile!" my mom would call out. I acquiesced from time to time, but mostly I was into striking my too-cool-for-school stares.

We spent a couple of hours out there, and then we were done. No mention of it for a couple of weeks until late September, my dad's birthday. It was a Sunday. We were all up, Dad, Mom, brother, and me, getting ready for the day. My mom brought out two wrapped packages and cheered, "Happy birthday Steve!" My dad put his cigarette in the side of his mouth, smiled, looked through the darkened lenses of his glasses, and said, "What's this?"

He tore off the brown paper wrapping the picture frames and just stared. Moving his head up and down, taking in the collection of photographs, resting on the big single shot of just my brother and me.

Oh, this is what that day at the park was all about? Right on. I was pretty proud, surprisingly, relative to my attitude the day of the photo shoot. My brother and I stood next to each other, wearing shit-eating grins. I couldn't tell what Dad was thinking. *Did he like them? Did we do good? Did my mom make the right call?* I was always nervous with that guy.

Finally, he gave us big hugs, and I relaxed. I figured we did all right. Phew.

"OK, boys, time to get to church," said my mom. My mom was a born-again Christian. We went to church at least three times a week. Sunday morning, Sunday evening and

Wednesday night. Without fail. We read the Bible on top of that. So going to church was just part of the routine. For the three of us, at least. My dad wasn't always in on the drill. He would fade in and out of the church deal, joining in for a few months, then taking a few months off. It was not comfortable for him, the God stuff or the pews or who knows what, because he always came out of church sweating like he was in a greenhouse in late July.

His birthday was not a day that he wanted to spend in church. Quickly his mood changed. "Why are you going to church?" he asked. He said we should stay home on his birthday.

My mom looked at him quizzically. "What are you talking about? We always go to church," she said. "If you don't want to come, that's your choice, but the boys and I are going to church."

That was it for the smiles and celebration. Didn't take much to set my dad off. He got in that pissed-off, bowed-up stance with his don't-even-think-about-fucking-with-me stare. It was scary. Popped in another cigarette and then just stared at the TV screen. He was gone. Just figuratively at this point. It was an all-too-common scene of my dad angry and my mother fretting. Off to church we went.

After church, we pulled into the carport on the side of our two-room-wide by two-room-deep little house. The lights were out. Drapes closed. From the outside, it looked as if no one was home. My mother, my brother, and I walked in the front door almost simultaneously, me a bit curious. My father was sitting in the chair immediately to the right of the door, cigarette smoke swirling throughout the room, a beer by his side. Lying there, in plain view, propped up on the couch in the center of the room, were the picture frames of my brother and me. Except there were no faces—just holes.

I stared. It was clear the faces had not been cut out with a pair of scissors. The shapes of the holes were not even. There were burn marks, the edges of the holes blackened and either curled in or curled out. The frames were still intact, so I knew what that collage had been originally, just a few hours before. Those holes had been created with a gun. *He shot my face out of the frame.*

My mom quickly scurried what was left of his birthday present out of the room. My dad took off. I couldn't hear if he said anything or not. I couldn't hear anything, couldn't see anything. I just stood there, dazed, already out of it, my mind quickly numbing. I then melted away, out into the yard.

It seems that all my childhood memories occur outside. I don't have many recollections of the inside of my home. I have wondered if it's because that's where my parents occasionally up, but mostly down, marriage occurred. There were fights. I remember one time there were broken dishes. I didn't ever see physical fighting, but I did see my mom's tears all too often.

I walked in on them having sex one time. Foreplay more precisely. The lights were on. I peeked for about two seconds and ran back into my bedroom as fast as I could. My parents didn't know I had seen them, or if they did, they didn't come to get me. I stared up at the bottom of the top bunk for a while, registering what I just saw. Did I see pride in my dad's face? How could she be doing that to him? She's an angel. He's a disgusting, smoking piece of shit. What did he do to her to get her to do that?

Sometime later, still in grade school, I came home, sat on the couch, and told my mom that I didn't want to manipulate people. My mom got this quizzical look on her face and came around to the couch, sitting next to me. "What?" she asked. "I don't want to manipulate people, Mom." Nothing more was said. She just hugged me, then left her arm draped around me as we sat in silence.

Eventually, there was the night my dad took off for good. Actually, really left us this time. I was thirteen years old, in seventh grade. No goodbyes, no warning. I just woke up one morning and my mom, in tears, told me Dad had left. In the middle of the night, he drove off to live with his brother in Oklahoma. That was it. No note. Gone.

My mom forced us to reach out to him. He wouldn't take our phone calls, so she had us record messages to him on cassette tapes instead. I'm not sure what I said or how many times we made recordings. I know I pushed back, thinking it was totally weird. I don't even know if he ever got them or listened to them. But I do remember that recorder we used to make the tapes. It was an old black tape recorder, about a foot long, with a handle that slid out the top and one speaker. It had those buttons that were hard to press down, especially when attempting to push record and play simultaneously.

I used it to record Casey Kasem's *American Top 40* off the radio as often as possible. I would post a "Recording in Process" sign on the door leading to my bedroom, which I thought of as my recording studio. I stretched one of the stereo speakers into my bedroom, leaned the little recorder against it, and recorded the radio station. It was FM radio, KRSB, the only station in town that I was aware of. There were a few inches of space between the speaker and the recorder. When the commercials were on, I hit stop then listened intently to the ads. As soon as that sweet voice came back on the air, I'd hit the play and record buttons at the same time, never letting the recorder get too far from the speaker.

With my dad finally gone-gone, I noticed my mom's life-changing. She became more focused, more organized, a list maker, a doer. She moved on to the next phase in her life. Just kept going. The hugs and smiles and laughter were still there, but out popped determination and perseverance as well.

She became less of just a mom and more of a leader. I became less of a son and more of a grown-up.

I got my first job, at age fourteen, through a welfare program my mom qualified for. For a summer, I rode my bike to either a local hospital or the high school to do landscaping work. My mom was not happy about it one bit, but what was she going to do? We didn't have any money. It was so embarrassing. I made sure to volunteer for the jobs in the backs of the buildings, away from any main road. Somehow, I was able to get myself and my bike to baseball practices and games also.

My mom decided to go back to school full-time at the local community college about ten miles away. She did really well. I saw a lot of A's at the top of her papers. I heard from her friends that her instructors said she added value to her classes. She was proud of that. It was hard on me, her being away or otherwise busy. But it made her feel good.

My best friend Brad's parents owned a medical supply business and gave my mom a job. Some kind of office/clerical position. They said she was a hard worker, learned quickly, and was an asset. They also added that she was always friendly.

That left me to fend for myself most of the time. I learned how to cook, do laundry and clean the house. None of it ever felt like a chore, though. I didn't question it or think it was unfair. It was just part of life. If I wanted my uniform clean for the game, I better do the laundry. If I wanted to eat, I should fix a meal.

After about two years, when I was in ninth grade, my dad showed up back in Roseburg. My parents were still married, but he didn't move back into the house. He found a crappy, run-down, depressing studio apartment above a strip mall out past the edge of town, where the blue-collar companies and auto wrecking yards existed. At first we would just visit him during the day, no staying the night. There were a couple of pieces of real furniture, plus stuff cobbled together acting as furniture— pallets or boxes or crates stacked up, that sort of thing. I wasn't angry at him, but I wasn't overjoyed to see him either. I just went with the flow. Time to see Dad. OK. Time to go home. OK.

Eventually, my dad upgraded to a duplex with room for my brother and me to spend the night. We would load up on junk food—GooGoo Cluster ice cream, Fig Newtons, Peanut Buster Parfaits from the Dairy Queen—maybe grab an Abby's pizza, and then watch movies. He had HBO! Michael Keaton and Tim Allen would make us laugh and laugh, then we would tell the jokes all over again after the show was over. He let me stay up till midnight, sometimes even later.

Except when he didn't want me.

My mom would get a call on a Friday afternoon and come to my room, in tears, to tell me my dad wasn't going to take me for his weekend. Sometimes she would try to come up with an excuse for him, but eventually, she would just give it to me straight. He said that he was just too busy. I never really knew why he didn't want me.

In my late thirties, I began having this recurring daydream. Except it was more of a nightmare. I imagined driving up to my house, ho-hum, in my easy, safe little suburb. Midway through the U-turn that I would take to get into my driveway, I would notice his lame red Camaro, with those stupid vanity plates, parked in front of the house. I pictured myself, walking up the stairs from the garage, hearing sobbing and rustling, and my dad yelling, "Shut the fuck up!"

Oh no. No, no, no. I knew it. This is not good. Damn him!

My dad would be sitting in our piano room at the top of the stairs with a gun and a smoke. My wife and kids would be across the room from him, sitting on the floor bound with duct tape on their wrists, feet, and mouth.

I walked through the front door and faced him. My dad would ask me how it felt now to have shut him out of my life. How did I feel about not calling him, visiting him? I would envision my wife crying, begging for help. My son and daughter screaming, "Dad! Dad! Help!" I wouldn't move. Staring at my dad. Shaking my head. Figuring out how I was going to get my family out of this.

In the next part of my vision, I turned around, not even acknowledging the situation. I was hoping that I would have that kind of courage to shock my dad. Completely ignore him once again, letting him know that finally, finally, after all of these years, I wasn't afraid of him. I was in my thirties and in shape. He was an out-of-shape, smoking, fifty-year-old. He no longer had control of me. I would just turn around and look for a solution.

I would go into the garage to get a weapon. I had hammers and knives and screwdrivers and crowbars. Dozens of potential weapons. I would take one tool that I could hit him with and another to stab him. Then I would head back up the stairs, not say a word, walk straight into his gun, and begin beating him by hammering down on his gun hand, then working my way all over his body. I would end it by skewering his gun hand to the ground with a heavy, sharp object. A huge Phillips screwdriver.

Then I would turn around and free my family. The end.

Following each of these visions, I would talk to myself, prepare myself for the day, try to convince myself just 1% further that I could actually do this. That I could garner up the strength and courage to actually see this through. Pull it off like Liam Neeson in a *Taken* movie. With every vision, I hoped I became stronger and more assured. I knew I would need tremendous confidence if I was ever going to take on my old man. Beat the shit out of him like I'd been dreaming about most of my adult life.

Though I was sure it was a possibility, I never had to find out.

Over the years, some light was shed on that rumor about my dad with the high school-age neighbor girl. The parents went to the same church as us. Bits and pieces of information just randomly surfaced. However, I never knew the girl personally since she was years older than me.

I didn't know what to think. Sure, it could have happened. My dad was a sonofabitch, after all. On the other hand, I didn't know anyone who would do something like that, and my brain couldn't even fathom it.

When I was in my early thirties, living in Atlanta, I got a call from my dad, still in Roseburg. I hadn't seen him in a while, and we weren't talking much.

He admitted to me that he forced himself on an underage girl. A girl I knew, very aware of his relationship with her, a different girl than that childhood rumor. *What does he say to these girls? What words does he use to get them to look past the smoky breath and angry glasses?*

Then … *Shit, it was all true.*

I paused, a long time, and then only said one thing, "Were you drunk?"

Hoping.

"No," he replied. My shoulders sank.

That was the last time we talked. I didn't want any part of that guy in my life. There were so many other great men in my life with whom I wished to deepen my relationship.

Based on the secondhand accounts I heard, the official death certificate probably said something about organ failure and/or cancer. The death certificate in my head lists the cause of death as anger.

CHAPTER 3

Drinking

The first time I got drunk, I did a bunch of shots, got stumbling-blackout wasted, hurled, and ended up bawling like a baby.

If that wasn't a sign of things to come.

It was the last day of my first year in high school, tenth grade. I was fifteen. I spent the school year mostly with seventeen- and eighteen-year-olds, playing varsity football and baseball, going to homecoming and prom with senior cheerleaders. The seniors' stories I heard on Mondays were a little different than what I talked about with my buddies the previous year in junior high. I had a close group of friends who, at the time, committed to never getting drunk, pondering how cool it would be to order milk at a bar. These new friends talked about the crazy things that happened on Friday and Saturday nights. By the time that last day of school rolled around, I had heard enough laughter and carrying on about how great these "parties" were, how drunk people got, or how crazy that guy or girl was. I just had to give it a try.

Plus, I had the perfect setup.

My dad lived by himself in this trashy little apartment up the hill from downtown, about a seven-minute drive from the high school. During journalism class, with nothing to do since the last paper had been printed, I grabbed a couple of the juniors, one of whom had a car, and we went up to my dad's. He was at work, and I knew where the hidden key was.

We got into the apartment and found the bottles of cheap liquor on the top shelf next to the fridge. All brown alcohol. My dad had a few cans of soda pop in the refrigerator—root beer, grape, lemon-lime, orange. I noticed it was the cheapest generic brand he could find, of course, as I shook my head. We pulled them all out, the cans and the bottles, got a few small glasses, and started experimenting. This booze with that soda. That booze with this soda. It was just awful tasting, but for months I'd been hearing about all the fun people were having at parties, so I just kept pouring 'em and downing 'em. Two, three, four drinks. Bam, bam, bam. How about milk in this one? Sure! No shot glasses or measurement tools. No idea about the ratios of alcohol to mixers one may find in a proper drink. Just pour and slam. Five, six, seven drinks. So many in less than thirty minutes. *Did they have as many drinks as me?*

I tried to clean up my dad's kitchen to hide our existence, but I was more concerned about getting back to school in time. We hightailed it back to the high school. By the time I got out of the car, I was drunk. It did not feel good, but I laughed anyway. *Holy shit. Is this what being drunk is?*

The only thing that needed to be done on the last day of school was to walk up to the teacher, turn in your textbook, and watch the teacher sign off that it had been returned. That was all I had to do for another four or five periods. I showed up to my next class and pulled it off. The alcohol was still working its way through my system, and I was getting progressively less functional. My friends started to notice, and the word was out that I was drunk. Really drunk. Friends carried me from class to class. They took my books to the teacher for me, saying I wasn't feeling well. I couldn't put together a sentence. I couldn't stand up straight.

At some point, my best friend, Brad, took me into the bathroom and slammed me against a stall. He was pissed. What the hell was wrong with me!? We didn't drink. Why did I go and drink? I laughed and mumbled how cool it was. He just shoved me down onto a toilet and walked out, disgusted.

I made it through the day without getting caught. No principal's office. No teacher scolding me. Someone gave me a ride home. Summer league baseball tryouts were at the ballfield across the main highway past the street I lived on. My high school coach was the coach of that team as well. I got word to him that I wasn't feeling good. Then I just walked around the neighborhood with a few girls. By late afternoon I felt like absolute shit. That's when the tears started flowing. It hurt so bad. I was throwing up. I was confused. *What had I done? Why did I feel like this?* The girls were laughing and consoling, letting me know everything would be just fine. The school year was over, and I didn't get in trouble.

My mom didn't find out. Eventually, my dad would, but he just thought it was funny. Seemed kind of proud of me, actually. Gave me a few tips on what I could have done differently. Hard liquor affects you differently than beer. Milk can help with an upset stomach, which is why there are so many drinks made with cream. The bottom of the glass leaves rings on the countertop. Mixing types of alcohol is terrible—just pick one and stick with it all night long. Being hungover sucks, huh?

Such was my father's advice.

With the taste of puke still fresh in my mouth, I stayed pretty light on the booze that summer, maybe a beer or two at the few parties I explored. I tried Kodiak, a mint-flavored, long-cut dipping tobacco popular with teenagers. I really didn't like that woozy kind of buzz. It wasn't until the move to Juanita that I really began to test the waters of my drinking abilities.

That school was full of partiers! Winners and partiers. Boys and girls drank after every victory, which is to say, they drank every weekend. They didn't need to fight for their right to party. They earned it. Roseburg sports, especially the football team, was all buttoned up. My mom gave me a traditional, Christian upbringing. I grew up learning that children obeyed adults, no questions asked. Keep your mouth shut and do what you are told. This new school did not feel like that at all. There was such a confident and carefree attitude at that school. What a new perspective for me.

One of the craziest things was that it seemed that someone's parents were out of town on vacation every weekend. *How do these people have the money to take all of these big trips? Don't they have jobs?* Their '70s style split-level suburban development homes seemed like mansions. One of them seemed to always be accommodating a party.

Scott had taken me into Seattle early in the year to get us fake IDs. In a tiny retail shop in Pioneer Square, we each filled out a card and gave it to the lady behind the counter. I went with an Oregon ID, Roseburg address, thinking that the more accurate I was, the more likely the ID would be accepted. I then had my picture taken. In a few minutes, we had a laminated card that was little more than a mother's note claiming, "He's twenty-one, I promise."

After that first Juanita party, I started to get my drinking legs under me. I found out relatively quickly that I was a good drinker. After more than a few beers and/or wine coolers, other kids were getting silly and falling over. I seemed to be upright and able to carry on a conversation.

With that prized skillset and the sports, I began to feel like I could fit in at my new school. The kids I looked up to all went to parties. They were the same kids in my advanced math and history classes and on my sports teams. The drinking was just part of being a Rebel.

When I came back to Roseburg after my mom died, I discovered that all of my nondrinking junior high buddies were also now drinkers. We had a good laugh at that one. Since my fake ID said Oregon on it, I felt pretty good about buying alcohol in my little hometown.

It's not like I had a lot of adult presence in my house when I moved in with my dad. That, too, didn't change much. I didn't have an adult in Kirkland after my mom took off and didn't have one in Roseburg with my dad. The bonus with him was that he actually thought drinking was cool. "Don't get any girls pregnant" was about the only partying rule he set with me. He kept cases and cases of cheap beer stacked up at the end of the hallway. "Only $5.99 a case! Picked up a few," he exclaimed as he put a couple cases of Hamm's on top of the cases of Meister Brau he bought the previous week.

The house parties were less prevalent in Roseburg, but we still found places to drink. Since my dad took off for Eugene every Wednesday night to see his girlfriend, I held poker parties with just a few kids involved. I never had any big parties at my dad's house. While I knew he was OK with me drinking, I wasn't too sure about how he'd feel about me having a party. So I would do what small-town kids do. Cruise the strip looking for trouble.

On the few occasions there were house parties, I was a lead dog. Corralling fellas to shotgun beers. Winning at quarters or whatever drinking game was being played. Sometimes it felt too easy.

My calculus class was a two-period block, separated by lunch. It was taught for college credit and structured like a college class, lecture then lab. On test days, it was review, lunch, test. One of my standard lunches was Taco Time. I would grab a couple of burritos—Crispy #2's as they were known back then—and an extra-large Mountain Dew, then head home.

Somewhere I read that alcohol was a depressant that calmed people down. When it came time to take one of my first calculus exams, I figured it would be a good idea to have one beer before the test to calm my nerves a bit. I ended up setting the curve with a ninety-eight out of one hundred. I tried beer again before the next test, except I went with two this time. I didn't set the curve, but I did get a score in the nineties, just a couple of points off the curve. *OK, that's good. Two beers, and I'm solid.* I ended up getting an A for the semester.

Since drinking while taking exams seemed to work for me, I figured drinking while working would as well. At the cemetery that was my summer job, the other workers and I would go get Big Gulp cups and beers on Friday afternoons. We would pour beers in the soda cups and drink while we mowed the grass or used the weed eater around the headstones.

When my dad was out of town one Saturday night, a buddy and I decided to try something stronger than beer, MD 20/20, commonly known as Mad Dog. The hardest stuff you could get at a little mini-mart at about thirty or forty proof. That malt liquor "wine" tasted absolutely horrible, even when mixed with juice or soda pop. But we downed a bottle each, then took the third bottle with us on the road. We headed out looking to steal street signs with girls' names that we wished would have liked us back. I wasn't sure what was supposed to happen after we got the signs, but it made sense as we headed out the door.

We found the first few signs were pretty well lighted, so we passed them by. After driving all over town, eventually finishing the third bottle, we finally found a worthy sign in a good location. Except we had no tools to remove the sign. After some pushing and pulling, then some kicking, we decide to just pull the whole thing out of the ground. Sign, pole, even the underground concrete the pole was attached to. Once we were back at the car, we realized it didn't fit in the trunk or the back seat. Unless …

We rolled down a window and hung the concrete out the window. Not the end with the sign on it. That would draw attention. We ended up at the elementary school parking lot in a neighborhood with a lot of cute girls. Once we opened the car's doors, the Def Leppard cassette blared through the streets. We were rockin' now!

It only took a few minutes for the blue and red lights to show up. We took off running, and I hid. It wasn't such a good hiding place because they found me before I could catch my breath. They walked me back to the parking lot, asking me a few questions. I couldn't hear a thing with the insides of my head swirling with confusion and fear. Maybe I should have given better answers because I was cuffed and stuffed.

A few minutes in the back of the cop car, with cuffs digging into my wrists, it occurred to me what was happening. I started crying. Begged them not to take me to jail. No words from the cop. He just put the car in drive and took off, me behind the plastic barrier. I was in the car for what seemed like forever. Finally, we ended up back in the same school parking lot where I was nabbed.

My dad knew the officer and was waiting for me. Small town, no jail time. Not even a ticket. They had a good laugh. My dad's fatherly advice for that one was, "If you're going to run from your own car, you better keep running."

That fall, I started at the University of Washington. I immediately joined a fraternity known as a jock, partying house. School was important, but beer and sports were cool. In my freshman class of thirty-five boys, thirty-four had a varsity letter in a high school sport. A few were competing for the UW.

Early on, my drinking prowess paid off once again. While other freshmen were passed out or puking, I hung with the upperclassmen. After doing a few shots with one senior, he told me: "You're all right. You can handle your alcohol."

In the fraternity, I could always find someone to drink with. It might be a different person each night, but in a house of one hundred guys, I always had a drinking buddy. Tuesday night was freshman night. On Wednesdays, we had parties with another sorority or two. Kegs were always around. Thursday night was cheap drinking at the bars, so I quickly obtained a better fake ID that could pass at bars. Friday and Saturday held some version of a party or just another night at the bars.

My priorities in college were, in order: partying, intramural sports, paying for college with odd jobs, grades, then, way down the list, learning.

I was really good at this drinking stuff. No matter my ranking in the classroom or on the playing field, which kept dropping as each month of college passed, I could be a top-tier drinker. I could win at that. Around any container of alcohol, I knew I could handle whatever challenge was put forth, competing with someone else, whether they knew it or not, or just testing myself. Eventually, this is all I cared about because I knew I wouldn't fail. I knew I wouldn't be a loser. Nothing worse than losing.

I never worried about my drinking while in college. Sure, I outdrank everyone I knew, but I didn't see it as a problem. I looked at it as a talent. But when I moved down to Orange County, California, right after college, I got a different perspective. One of my roommates was not a partier. The other would party every once in a while, but he was an engineer who had a demanding job, so it wouldn't get too out of control. We would go out on weekends from time to time and meet up with a group of his buddies from college to drink, but that was about it. With my cushy job and tolerance level, I was ready to go out just about every night.

That's when I became comfortable heading out drinking by myself. It wasn't too long before I became comfortable getting wasted by myself.

In the beginning of my time in Orange County, I was more adventurous. During the day, driving around Orange County working my sales territory, I would make mental notes of bars I wanted to check out. Surfer bars in Newport. Honky-tonks in Tustin. Clubs in Irvine. I would visit them as soon as I had the chance.

Eventually, all of that scouting and driving around became too much work. Plus, I didn't want to put in the effort to meet people who were there more for the socializing than the alcohol. A little joint across the street from my apartment complex, Jasper's, ended up being my go-to bar during the week.

Jasper's was your typical strip mall dive bar with greasy food, a pool table, and a long bar, with a few round tables scattered about. It smelled like french fries, smoke, and Crown Royal. After a few visits, I began recognizing a few of the regulars. Enough for a head nod. Occasionally I talked with a waitress or two, but I was mostly there for the cheap booze and easy atmosphere.

All too often, I would close the place down and want to continue drinking. Have to continue drinking. I couldn't go back to the apartment and wake my roommates up, so I began stashing bottles in my car. I would stumble through the parking lot to my car, sip whiskey from the bottle, and flip between country music stations, periodically revving up the engine so the battery wouldn't die on me.

While listening to George Strait sing about feeling blue the day he lost someone, sadness and grief would just engulf me. I lost Mom and Todd, Roseburg and Juanita. I would drink and cry, then drink some more and cry some more, alone in my company-provided black Pontiac Grand Prix. Merle Haggard would jump right in the seat beside me, singing how the bottle let him down because he couldn't drink enough to keep someone off his mind. Dwight Yoakam crooned—"it never hurts except when I cry."

When my emotions started to get really bad, when I just couldn't stop crying, I drove my car to the most remote, darkest spot of the apartment complex. I turned the music up as loud as I could. There I could let country music and a bottle of whiskey prop me up as my tears flowed down.

When I moved back up to Seattle to try and get into the software industry, the house I moved into with Scott and Steve was in the neighborhood where I began my drinking career, and in the same metropolitan area as most of my fraternity brothers, with whom I had established my drinking bona fides. I was coming back!

Seattle in the mid-1990s was the epicenter of cool. Starbucks was just taking off nationwide. Red Hook Brewery was a leader in the microbrewery movement. Microsoft and the dotcoms were happening. And grunge.

I was a sales guy for a startup software company, traveling on business a lot at the time. When I would mention I was from Seattle, anyone within earshot would be interested. Pearl Jam? Nirvana? Doc Marten boots? Flannel? Dark coffee and dark beer? Was all of that true? What was it like? Do you know Eddie Vedder?

I had a couple of key topics of conversation. A good friend's brother was in an up-and-coming band. I spent a lot of time near the apartment complex where the movie *Singles* was filmed.

"Hey, this guy is from Seattle," someone would say. Instant friends. Better yet, drinking buddies. Between the trendiness of Seattle and my aptitude for barroom games, no matter what town I was in, I could always find someone to drink with. There was always a guy who would get drunk enough to give me the old "I love you man" toward the end of the night.

I started to make a little money with the second software company I worked for. I moved from Schmidt's in a can and shots of Cuervo Gold to single malt scotch and Manhattans.

I really got into whiskey. My first drink as a twenty-one-year-old with my grandpa was a Dewar's and soda. My mom's maiden name comes from a county in Ireland. Scotland has a county called Andrews. I began researching and buying books about scotch. I learned about the geography of Scotland distilleries, the water, the distilling process. It opened my eyes to a whiskey lifestyle, complete with leather chairs, cigars and driving shoes. I thought it was fun to share all of this with my friends. "This is a highland malt, which means … blah, blah, blah." Or, "You should try your old fashioned with rye whiskey because … blah, blah, blah … " With all my enthusiasm over this brown liquor, which few my age seemed to really like, people around me would give it a try, even the girls.

Drinking was also my way of exploring Seattle's nightlife. I would hop from a music venue to a backdoor lounge to a late-night club, drinking whatever I felt was the appropriate drink for the venue. I never got tired from drinking. Never passed out. By this time, I never threw up either. I kept going and going through last call and straight to someone's house for a few early morning cocktails. Thursday, Friday and Saturday nights were standard drinking nights, along with other nights if I wanted to see a ballgame or a band. Always drinking before, during, and after.

Drinking was part of my life. Since I was good at it, really good at it, I thought it was what I was built for. It was the thing I felt recognized for. One thing I could be "The Best" at. I continued to drink heavily multiple days a week throughout my twenties. Eventually, the novelty of the new scene, the new neighborhood, or the latest place or craze finally wore off. I was left with just the drinking. I still enjoyed all of the variety the city had to offer. Still looked for new and interesting outings, but those became the backdrop. They were just the setting. Getting drunk was the main act.

In my late twenties I met my wife at Visio, a rising software startup in downtown Seattle. She was just an intern, in her last year at the UW, so dating wasn't supposed to happen. But I couldn't help myself. After a few months of being around her, I became attracted to something beyond her looks, beyond even her thinking. It was an air of confidence and optimism that pulled me in. So, as she was finishing her school year, with some prodding by buddies at work, I asked her out.

It was supposed to be a summer fling. She was a hottie with an adventurous spirit and a fun attitude. Both of us thought we could go on summer road trips together, maybe the occasional wedding or party, and that was going to be it.

I had no idea I was going to fall in love. But, after a couple of weeks of spending nearly every nonworking hour with her, I knew she was going to be The One, a feeling that completely blindsided me.

I decided to invite her to the Prosser Food and Wine Festival in eastern Washington. A buddy grew up in Sunnyside, a little town next to Prosser, and a big group of guys had been to the festival in summers prior. It was a bold move, inviting a girl in the middle of that crew, but I was secure with us and confident she could handle it.

After drinking all day at the festival, followed by shots and beers at a dive bar or two, a few of the dudes hopped in the back of someone's rig. I went for the steering wheel because, clearly, I was the best drinker and driver.

Sandy stopped me in my tracks as I approached the steering wheel. Then she had the keys. *How did she do that!?* I knew she hadn't drunk as much as me, and might actually be sober. *Weird.*

Quickly … *What the hell? What is she doing!? Didn't she know I was the best drunk driver of the bunch?* This rig was a jacked-up four-by-four. She was maybe five-three. She wasn't going to be able to handle that thing. I knew what I was doing driving a rig in a country town. All of the fellas were fine with it. This is what we did. How dare she get in the middle of that? But she did. We butted heads for a while, while the crew looked on in awe. She didn't back down. She ended up driving us all home and impressing everyone that night, especially me.

Once summer ended, she was off on a six-month cruise around the world as part of Semester at Sea, a college-accredited learning experience that would be her final set of classes in college. She began in Vancouver, British Columbia, and had her first stop in Japan. Somehow, we found a way to communicate through letters and international phone calls during her first few weeks away. But it didn't ease my longing for her. I needed to see her, and lucky for me, she said she needed to see me too. She let me know that Egypt would be her longest stayover. So we agreed. I would meet her in Egypt.

I hadn't been anywhere. I had just begun to see some of the major cities in the U.S. I went to Mazatlán for my high school senior trip, but I wouldn't say we experienced Mexico. Yet here I was hopping on a plane, by myself, traveling halfway around the globe, just to meet this girl I'd dated for about ten weeks. I still couldn't believe it. Chalked it up to love.

We had a magical, educational, and revealing six days in Cairo, Alexandria, Giza, and the highways between. Six sleepless nights overlooking the Nile River. We said goodbye in Port Said as she boarded the ship headed for Greece. For me, though, it was, *see you soon*. After that week, I knew. I just knew.

When she got back to Seattle, we acknowledged that the deepening of our relationship was incredible, but it was happening too quickly. We agreed that we needed to put down some roots. We dated for over a year. Then were engaged for almost a year after I stumbled through a proposal on the white sand of Siesta Key, Florida.

We both were in software and had early success in our careers. We both grew up in the Pacific Northwest. I had done some traveling. She had done more. Once we were married, in January 1999, with our thirties creeping upon us, we started thinking about living somewhere besides the Northwest. We casually discussed international opportunities with different companies. We made some half-hearted attempts at landing a gig, but it felt like a stretch for both of us to get a job abroad in the same city at the same time. So we decided to focus on the U.S.

Even though we liked Chicago and Boston, we didn't want to move to the Midwest or Northeast. The winters were too harsh. We wanted someplace warm. And, though we both loved California, it was crossed off the list because we both felt we had a good understanding of that state. That left the South, which for us meant somewhere between Austin and Raleigh-Durham.

I figured that if I really wanted to make a run in the software industry, I would need more technical chops. I decided to apply to a few MBA programs that had a focus on information systems, one of which was Georgia Tech in Atlanta. I went to an old boss of mine asking for a reference for my application. Instead, he offered me a job based in Atlanta. *Make money, or spend money?* Make money it was. My wife was with Microsoft, which had a good-sized office in Atlanta. She figured she could get a transfer down there, so away we went.

―――

When I first moved to Atlanta, waiting for Sandy's internal transfer, I lived with my wife's aunt and uncle in a suburb north of the city. During this time, about six months, my drinking slowed down quite a bit since I didn't know anyone to go out drinking with. However, when I did drink, I drank like I always did—until I couldn't drink anymore.

One Saturday evening, when my aunt and uncle were out of town visiting one of their four kids, I made the shortest drive I could to my local strip mall dive bar. It wasn't a complete dump, with newish furniture and live music. I would give any place a try for at least an hour if it had live music. I bellied up to the bar and ordered Bud Light and a shot of Jack.

Sometime after midnight, I drove back to the house, stopping at a grocery store for a bottle of Jack Daniel's. Time to get really wasted and let myself go. That's how I was viewing drinking at this point.

I grabbed a glass of ice and headed up to my home office to put on country music and start the spiral. The first glassful tasted pretty good, so I poured another and switched back and forth between rockin' country to pop country to alt-country. By the end of the second glass, my tongue was getting pretty worn from the whiskey. I knew it was time to call it quits. Except I had the house to myself. No way I was stopping now.

I shifted the tunes to the sad stuff, any country song about leaving and losing. Tears started flowing. *Where was everybody!? Todd. Mom. Dad. Why did they all leave me? Why aren't they here with me!?*

I poured a third drink. It tasted awful, but I needed to feel the pain. I deserved to feel the pain. *Drink more!* I looked at that bottle of Jack Daniel's. "FUCK YOU!" I yelled, straight at that black label with the number seven, and took another pull as tears rolled down my cheeks. *Why did you leave me!?* It tasted like shit, but I was supposed to feel like shit. Another shitty swallow. Another song to make me cry.

Eventually, I couldn't down another one. I tried more ice. My mouth just couldn't handle another drop. *What a pussy!* I stumbled down to my bed and passed out, fully clothed, on top of the bedspread.

In August of that year, my wife's transfer came through. We bought a home in the midtown Atlanta neighborhood Virginia Highlands. With no children, two incomes, and the points and miles that came with two jobs that included regular travel, my wife and I took advantage of our freedom. We traveled all over the South—New Orleans to Miami to Charlotte. The Caribbean was just a two-hour flight. When not out of town, we explored our lively neighborhood full of restaurants, bars, and music venues. All within walking distance from our house. As always, I kept my eye out for cool-looking bars or potential places for live music.

I didn't hide my drinking from my wife, but I didn't really need to. She wasn't much of a partier and could fall asleep early, anywhere. I was never a day drinker. So most of the time, when I was drinking up a storm, I was without her. If we did start the evening together, out for dinner or having drinks, she would head home early and hit the sack. I would either drink by myself at home, content with my music and whiskey, or quietly head out the back door and find the nearest watering hole. Too many nights it was both.

One night, Sandy had to go out of town on business, leaving me free to explore on my own. Hell, I might as well be in college again! First stop—Buckhead. I went to a couple of places that I had visited years earlier when in Atlanta on business trips from Seattle. Most of the drinking places that attracted me had large outdoor drinking areas, which still felt so novel coming from the rainy Pacific Northwest. But, it wasn't too long before I felt a bit old for Buckhead and saw all I needed to see on my visit down memory lane, so I found my car and drove south back to my hood.

As I got out of Buckhead, I came to a fork in the road. Literally. I could veer right to Ponce, check out an open-air bar that looked like it might have live music and this other dive bar under an old hotel that I'd read about. Or, I could veer left, get my car back in my driveway, then safely walk around the corner to the blues music joint Blind Willie's.

With every spin of the wheels, I contemplated.

Go home and get out of the car. You are hammered.

No, suck it up. You're fine.

Sandy's not home. I absolutely gotta check these places out. Veer right it was.

Just as I drove over an overpass, I saw a bunch of lights ahead. *Sonofabitch. Some jackass got in an accident. I'm out.*

This was a sign. Time to go home. I made a U-turn, which I thought was quite a ways out from the spinning blue and red.

Except, suddenly, the lights were following me.

Holy crap. Cops. Quick, pull over, park behind the building, throw your keys out the window, fake like you're asleep.

That lasted about fifteen seconds.

"Outta the car," they yelled.

What? Huh? When I opened my eyes, it felt like half of the Atlanta police force was surrounding my car. *Well, that acting performance didn't work.*

The cops asked me many times, "Would you like to take a Breathalyzer test?" Nope. No way. Nope.

Never take the Breathalyzer. Isn't that what people said? No proof, no conviction.

I stayed strong. No Breathalyzer test for me.

"Well, let me see you walk," one of them said.

I'm an athlete. The best drinker I know. This will be easy.

After about seven steps, they walked me over to the paddy wagon, locked me in, and drove me down to the slammer. The Atlanta City Detention Center.

By this time, the alcohol and confusion had sunk in, and I was completely hammered. When I came to, I was in a jail cell with about a dozen other guys. *Just don't make eye contact. If you have to, you better throw the first punch. Please don't let it come to that.*

A few hours later, my brain started working. *Holy shit.* What was I going to do? How was I going to get out? No one was coming for me. I wasn't going to call anyone I knew, which was all of about two people in this new town of mine. No one in a uniform told any of us in the cell what to expect next. Eventually, I noticed a list of bail bonds outfits with phone numbers up on the wall outside the cell. I worked my way to a touch-tone phone on the wall and tried to dial the correct numbers. Miraculously, a live person answered. They would come down and get me. Just wait.

They handed out sandwiches. Mine smelled like tuna fish. I gave it to the guy next to me. *Maybe now I won't get beat up*. Finally, my name was called. I was out of the building and walking to a bail bonds shop. I paid $2,500 without even asking a question. Took a cab home and passed out.

Sandy was coming home that evening. I woke up in the afternoon, grabbed the spare keys to my truck, and took a cab to the road I thought I might have parked on. I had the driver go slowly up and down the street. "There it is!" I exclaimed. The driver dropped me off, and I found that my keys had been left on my seat. The door was open, but the pickup was fully functional. Nothing stolen. So lucky.

I drove to the airport with my tail between my legs. How was I going to explain this to Sandy? What an idiot I was. I met her in the terminal. We chit-chatted and started walking back to the pickup. We made it to the parking garage, then to my car. I stopped. I told her she should drive. She looked at me funny but said OK. The minute we were both in the car, I started crying and spilled my guts.

I was embarrassed. I felt bad because this was going to cost us money. Because I was drinking and driving. Because I was a jackass.

She didn't say anything.

Eventually, as she started the car, she said, "We'll get through this," as she patted me on the knee. I repeated how sorry I was, how stupid I was, over and over, through the tears. It seemed to me like she was just processing it all. She was a planner, forward-thinking and almost always rational, unlike me, who was constantly looking back.

After fifty hours of community service and a few thousand dollars in legal fees, it was over. No one in the neighborhood knew. My boss didn't know. I was still married.

A couple of years later, a little birthday celebration for me included some of my wife's family. Everyone had a Jack Daniel's whiskey-related gift for me. Sign. Cookbook. T-shirt. I was thirty-five years old. I had a great job with an established software company. I had made a successful transition to Atlanta. I was playing rec basketball and softball and running half-marathons.

All they saw was a drinker. Or maybe that's what I felt like looking at the gifts. Just an awful feeling. Did they really think that Tennessee whiskey was my hobby, my only interest, my favorite thing in life? *Seriously, is this what I am to them? Is this how they see me?* It bothered me so much, but I couldn't let it show. I was a damn good Jack drinker.

This was one of the first times I looked at my drinking negatively. Such a new concept, my mind couldn't really process it. A negative feeling for sure, but not strong enough to hold me back from downing Jack.

Into my mid- or late-thirties, I was able to drink only when I was "up"—ready for a party, in a good mood, in some kind of a celebratory mood. I never started the evening drinking because I was down, or stressed, or needed relief from life. I didn't start my night by drinking to get away from anything. It was always about finding fun because things were good, and I knew they would only be getting better as the party rolled on.

Eventually, though, sometime toward my late-thirties, I began to drink for no reason at all. I just didn't feel like doing anything else. I would pour half a glass of scotch or bourbon and just sit there sipping it, early in the evening, just after work, with no plans of going out.

I knew this was a bad sign.

Prior to this period in my drinking life, no matter how sad or angry I was at the end of a night of drinking, I could tell myself that I started out with good intentions. That the first six or ten drinks were all good. I could justify the later sadness or anger by telling myself that I had reasons for feeling dark. I started off in a good place, so it was all good. Plus, I would mostly wait until I was alone, or only with one or two close people, before I let the shit hit the fan. What harm was there, really?

But this? This type of drinking got me thinking, for the first time really thinking—what was I doing?

By the time I was transitioning from my midthirties to my late-thirties, every drunken night ended in tears or frustration. One or the other, just about guaranteed. In my early thirties, it only happened periodically. In my twenties, very seldom. By my late thirties, I was stuck between agonizing over how I should feel and how I did feel. I was stuck between a positive spin on my life up to that point and a negative one. A piece of me would look at all the losses I endured as strengthening.

I had made it through all of that and consider ... *Hey, look at me now. What a success I am. I have a great wife, plenty of money, awesome friends, amazing kids, we get to travel, I'm running half-marathons. Look at how strong I must be to have persevered and prevailed. I am a winner. I am awesome. I am owning life.*

Then, like spectators' faces at a tennis match, my thinking would switch to ... *Life is so fucked up. Why did all of this have to happen to me? Why is life so hard? My dad is a sonofabitch. My mom and my friends are gone, forever. Why did they have to die?*

On nights when I wasn't drinking heavily, I would get upset that I could only have one or two because "social drinking" was the proper way to behave in the setting. Or I had to drive with someone else in the car. Or I had to be up early for the kids. Whatever the reason, my insides churned at the idea of stopping drinking before I was done. So I saw those life commitments as "getting in the way" of my partying. Which was to say they were getting in the way of what I wanted to do. It was a sign of weakness that I couldn't do both.

I was no longer drinking to celebrate or for any other positive reason. I was drinking because I felt I had to. Like I had no choice. The result of this train of thought should have been obvious. I had a choice. I could have stopped drinking. I did not, which felt like an awful choice, but it was the only one I knew how to make. Such turmoil and loathing with every night of drinking. It was so draining. The constant internal arguments, and questions, and justifications, covered up with my Party Blue costume.

Eventually, the time came when I actually did want to stop drinking. I knew I had to. Not subconsciously, or sometimes. Staring me right between the eyes all the time. When I drove out of the driveway on my way to drink. As I went through those first, second, and third drinks, I knew where things were heading. I genuinely did want to give it up.

It wasn't helping any of the other pieces of my life that mattered to me. It was actually a huge hindrance. I ate like shit when I was drunk, then ate just as bad hungover. After a night of drinking, the best I could muster was about thirty minutes of non-sweating exercise. Most of the time, I just bailed on attempting to move my body altogether.

I was a less effective parent. Drinking time was time away from my kids to get drunk. Hungover meant not having good energy to be the type of parent I wanted to be. I couldn't support my wife, even truly be there with her.

It took away from my ability to advance my career and start my future business. I couldn't be as efficient a salesperson.

I drove drunk. All the time. Never occurred to me to take a cab. Somehow that was a waste of money. Besides, after a night of drinking, I knew I was a great drunk driver.

I spent such an incredible amount of money on my drinking. Experimenting. Stocking the bar and then wasting even more money after I was hammered. CDs. Clothes. Ridiculous man-cave-in-the-garage level décor. Shots for everyone I saw. Shots for people I had trouble seeing through my drunken stupor. Regretful spending.

Every time I got drunk, I felt worse about myself. I was weak. I didn't have the strength to be 100% when I wasn't partying, and I didn't have the power to just give it up. Just once, don't drink. Just tell whomever I was with that I was taking the night off. Or maybe even turn down a night out on the town. Just say, "Nope. I'm focusing on my family tonight and this weekend." Or "I have a big workout planned tomorrow. I'll pass."

I didn't know what I would be without the partying. I wasn't really good at anything else anymore. I was just another suburban dad with two kids. *Who would be my friend if I wasn't leading the drinking brigade? How would anyone like me if I wasn't awesome at something? How could I like me if I wasn't the best in the room at something?*

What would life even be like if I wasn't drinking?

It had consumed me for over twenty years. I couldn't imagine life without alcohol. I could not visualize an entire month without getting drunk. I was sure I could go for a week. But multiple weeks in a row? In my head, no matter what image or vision I created, I couldn't see it. My soul couldn't color in that person, even though my head had the outline.

And there was no way I could just cut back. I scoffed at that. One drink? Who are you kidding? What the hell is one drink? That's the stupidest idea I'd ever heard. What is the purpose of one drink? Let's go grab "a" beer. … Who does that?

Besides, I had tried that around age thirty. Like every good alcoholic, I went through the phases of slowing down. No drinking during the week. No drinking the brown liquor. No drinking after midnight. Only drink once a week. Only beer and wine.

The common, singular focus about this "solution" was that drinking was the focus. Not a replacement. Coming up with a solution that included the problem didn't get me very far.

Every day I battled. Myself. I fought with me. Who I thought I wanted to be vs. who I thought I was. There was no way I could tell someone else these thoughts. That would show weakness, would mean I was a loser. I would never admit these struggles to Sandy or a friend. Sandy was so competent in every area of her life. How could I let her know I couldn't handle the drinking anymore? Besides, who was smarter than me to figure it out? I knew what I needed to do. I was just weak. I just had to suck it up and bear down. Quit being a pussy. No one could fix that for me. I walked through the days, kicking myself and falling down, then kicking myself along the ground. I looked at my weak self and shook my head in disgust.

The feeling I had the night I yelled "fuck you" to a bottle of Jack Daniel's became more of a regular occurrence than an oddity. Making drinking harmful. I would drink until it stopped tasting good, and then I'd drink more. Force one more down. I'd drive as fast as I could, seventy on a thirty-five mph road coming back from last call at The Little Red Hen, hoping to catch air on one of the hills, thinking in the back of my mind that if I crashed, so be it.

I couldn't figure out why I was so conflicted about not drinking.

Obviously, not drinking meant being healthier. Why would I choose to drink? Even worse, how could I view other areas of my life as a conflict to drinking? Time with my kids. My relationship with my wife. My career. That I was conflicted about what should have been an obvious choice and solution added to my grief. What kind of man couldn't make that choice? There was this little piece of my conscience that knew the correct answer. But I couldn't make it. So instead, I ruminated only on the obstacle and drank it in.

CHAPTER 4

Scoreboard

When I was about five years old, I grabbed two sides of a checkerboard, lifted it above my head, flinging the pieces around the room. I then brought it down, smack, right across the bridge of my friend's nose. Because I lost. He was older than me, but still, he beat me.

As far back as I can remember, I had been a bad loser. I liked getting A's but absolutely hated getting B's. It felt great to answer a question correctly, but that feeling was gone the minute the bell rang. On the other hand, I couldn't fall asleep that night if my answer was wrong. In sports, I played not to lose. Not to get beat. Not to let the ball get past me.

The basis for my competitive spirit was established on a fear of losing. Unfortunately, that attitude worked out pretty well for me.

I won spelling bees and geography contests. In honors, advanced-placement and college-credit classes, I was closer to a 4.0 than a 3.5. I was above the ninety-fifth percentile in my college tests and even hit the ninety-ninth in one category.

I had a short-lived sports career, never playing a second of college ball. However, during that formative time in my life, I was an above-average athlete. Awards in baseball, tennis, basketball, football, and track. Eight varsity letters. Captain of a couple teams. A few all-league votes in high school football and baseball. Part of many winning teams, including a state champion football team, a 17-1 basketball team, a baseball team ranked number one in the state.

Every activity, every day, was a competition, a ranking. Practice. Games. Homework. Tests. I thrived on not losing. Even after my formal playing days were behind me, I found ways to compete. There were times in my twenties, playing on less organized teams in less organized leagues, that I was part of successful squads, giving me hope that I was still an athlete. Intramural championships at the UW. A couple of rec league softball championships. A club league basketball championship.

When I got to college, I no longer looked at grades as competition. The only goal I had was to get a college degree. At a big public institution like the UW, that wouldn't be a problem. No way I could fail, so I figured I didn't need to compete.

Beyond that, "get a degree," I had no purpose or plan. No idea what I wanted to do after college. The general thinking at the time, 1987, was that if you had your bachelor's degree, you were on your way to a good job. So I left it at that.

Drinking, on the other hand, well, that had immediate benefits. I thought it would make me cool. A leader. Lead dog in front of the pack. Besides, it didn't take long to realize that no one was going to beat me when it came to drinking.

Once I was able to make it into bars, with a fake ID initially, I naturally gravitated toward barroom games as well. Pool mostly. Some darts. There were many days that I spent more time on the fraternity pool table than I did on the UW campus. I didn't become the best in the house, although on some days I was.

Pool was also a game that I could just play alone. Competing against myself. I spent hours practicing bank shots, breaking and spinning the cue ball. Like I did back home in Roseburg, I could lose myself in little games. How many could I make in a row? Could I set up the next shot? Could I make a tough angle from across the table?

I would realize the benefits at the dive bars I went to. Drinking and a skills contest. Right up my alley.

One of the local TV stations would hold Clint Eastwood Week each spring, showing a different movie each night of the week. One of the few rooms in the fraternity with a TV, The Black Velvet Room, hosted that week on their TV. That room derived its name from the BV billboard covering its walls and ceiling. On Sunday night, as ten or so guys gathered to watch the first movie, I did some quick math in my head and decided it would be a good week to drink 1,000 ounces of beer. A half case of beer is 144 ounces. Seven times 144 is just over 1,000. It was only twelve cans of beer a day. Shouldn't be a problem.

I completed my goal by Friday night.

While pre-functioning for a sorority dance one spring, a small group of fellas from different fraternities got together in the pantry of the home of one of the girls. The pantry was as big as some of the rooms in my fraternity. One of the other frat guys brought in a half-gallon of cheap booze. "Here, take a pull," one of them said. The first guy took a short, sissy pull. We called him out. "You're batting ninth," someone said. Game on. "OK, starting lineup. Let's go." Someone else took a bigger pull. "That's a solid number two in the order."

The bottle went around, and each person was assigned a spot in the order based on the length of the drink. When it came to me, I passed. "I'll go last," I said. One of the guys I knew to be a strong drinker gave me a look that said, "right on." After everyone else had their turn, I took the half-gallon and said, "Let me know when I'm batting cleanup." I tipped the bottle back and kept an eye on everyone's faces. Their eyes grew. Gulp, gulp. Grew even larger. Gulp, gulp. Finally, someone said, "OK, OK, you got cleanup. Cleanup." I put the bottle down to cheers, shoulder punches, clapping, and whooping it up.

Every spring, the fraternity would hold Senior Week. This was a time for the younger classes to honor and celebrate the seniors, and for the seniors to bond one last time before heading out into the real world. Each night was a different function. All of the events involved drinking, but two specifically revolved around drinking.

There was the big-brother, little-brother half-case race. Each team consisted of two people, a senior plus one of his fraternal little brothers. The team had a half-rack of Rainier tall-boys (twelve sixteen-ounce beers), and the goal was to drink it as fast as possible. The first team to down all twelve beers won. My team won in about five minutes, with me drinking seven of the beers.

Another event was the Lambda mile. Another two-person team, but this was seniors only, and you could pick your partner. The race started at a bar at one end of University Avenue, better known as "The Ave." It was about a block off campus and housed the school's main strip of retail shops, restaurants, and bars.

Each team would drink a pitcher of beer. When all teams were done, we would jog together up to another bar and down another pitcher each. Then we would jog up to the far end of The Ave and down another pitcher. The race started when all teams finished their third pitcher. We all looked at each with some hesitation, thinking, "Are we really going to do this?" Once properly psyched up, we agreed it was time and said, "Go!" It was one mile, almost exactly, down a winding hill, to the final bar. The race was to get to this third bar and down a pitcher first. I was part of the winning team in that event also.

One summer weekend after my junior year in college, about twenty of us went to the Gorge to see Tom Petty. The Gorge at George is a hillside amphitheater that overlooks a canyon created by the Columbia River about a two-hour drive east from Seattle, a very remote part of the state. It is one of the most stunning concert venues in North America. A must-see for any live music fan. The stage is set such that the artists are facing east with their backs to the river. Music starts during the heat of the day and finishes well after dark. This part of eastern Washington is remote high desert. When the sun is out, it gets real hot. When the sun goes down, it gets real dark. As the lineup progresses to the headliner, the sun drops, and the scenery behind the music changes color with the setting sun. The reds and oranges turn to yellows, then gray, until finally, the sky is the darkest of blue with tiny pinpricks of starry whites in the night sky.

A good friend grew up just a short drive from The Gorge, so a bunch of us crashed at his parents' place for the concert. Enough guys and gals were drinking cold beer in the heat of the summer that we reasoned a keg was appropriate. After my second red Solo Cup, I checked the time and made a quick calculation. I could probably beat the twenty-four beers that a fraternity brother had downed on a recent fishing trip. I told myself I was going to drink thirty beers that day. I let everyone know my goal.

Attaboy Blue! Go for it! I like it! Confirmation I was going to be The Man.

I found a Sharpie pen and made tally marks on my left forearm for each beer, like a notch on the stock of a rifle. I made a sixth diagonal line with plenty of time to spare.

As I grew older, the opportunities to prove myself on the playing field became harder to find, and the alcohol games I made up for myself made less and less sense. Still, there was that urge to compete I couldn't shake. To measure myself against someone else. To check the score. In my head, life was a giant tournament. Advance or go home. I needed something to put up on my scoreboard. So, I found a new way to assess myself.

Money.

In late 1995, at age twenty-six, the company I was working for went public. I finally had some dough. Not Vocational Freedom money. But enough money to pay cash for a car. To put a down payment on a house. To pay off all of my student loans and still have enough left over to start a retirement fund. No more bounced checks, which happened more than once in college. No more debt. My dad always said, "never owe anyone any money." A massive burden had been lifted.

I was in another world. I was checking out the stock market. Subscribing to *Money* and *Fortune* magazines. Buying decent clothes. A couple of years later, I caught another break when I landed my first six-figure salary job.

I was winning again.

Just after my dad took off, when I was thirteen, my mom was driving this beat-up, rusty, brownish-orangish Volvo. The driver seat was kept up by bricks, which weren't too different a color than the car's exterior. There were two bricks, and they would wiggle off balance from time to time, falling and cracking, so we'd have to readjust them to keep the front seat from falling into the back. That Volvo was touch-and-go. Worked most of the time, but not all the time. My mom said a prayer every time we hopped in the car and she turned the key, then another every time the light turned green.

We were forced to go on food stamps. My mom dropped out of college to have me. We lived in a shrinking town. Even when she did land a minimum wage job, we had to scrape together some change on the day before payday just to get some calories. Still, there were times when our cupboards were bare. Literally bare. Not often, but enough. It's a heart-stopping feeling to open the fridge and see nothing in it. Then search every inch of the kitchen cabinets and not see anything edible. Not an "I don't feel like eating what I'm seeing" kind of empty. Empty-empty.

We had a closet in the hallway, in which a couple of shelves were used for food storage. Each was a little taller than a jar of spaghetti sauce high and about my arm's length deep. On one of those really empty days in the kitchen, my brother and I remembered Mom stashed some food in the hall closet. Hopeful, we went out and opened a cabinet door, but we couldn't see any food in there either. *There has to be something.* I stuck my arm back as far as I could and felt a jar. Pulled it out and saw it was some canned cherries that my grandma made for us.

Now, with something to work with, we took a different look through the kitchen and discovered a bit of stale bread left in the back of a drawer. There's a meal in there somewhere. We each took a few cherries and a knife and started slicing up the cherries. Cherry sandwiches are what we ate that day.

We also ate a lot of government cheese around that time. Government cheese was this five-pound block of processed cheese, closer to Velveeta than Tillamook Cheddar, which the government would periodically hand out to those of us on welfare. My mom would be embarrassed when the announcement came that some was available to the poor folk. She would sit on the couch and fret, in disbelief that her life had come to this, trying to comfort us by telling us that it was OK, not so bad. Eventually, she would get up and drive over to get her handouts. She commented under her breath that she hoped no one would see her. Then she would giggle, as if that would matter, which was as comforting as anything she ever said. She would head out anyway, to some nondescript building, stand in line, and come back with food.

We melted cheese on anything that would hold it, all day for days at a time if we had to. The whole situation was weird, but that cheese was delicious. I had no problem eating it for every meal, over and over, on crackers and bread and tortillas. It was food. How could I get sick of it?

On payday or coupon day, we hit the grocery store. After putting food in the grocery cart and making our way to the register, my mom would begin loading the counter in order of priority. Milk and bread first. Grape jelly toward the back.

She would watch them ring up each item, calculating it against all the money she had in the world. If the total got too big, she would back out that last item and call it good.

When she didn't do the math quickly enough, or when every item was a priority, I would watch her look into her billfold, then watch her shoulders sink. That meant she didn't have enough money. She would flip through a couple of dividers to the food stamps. I could see tears were welling up in her eyes. I couldn't grasp what she was actually feeling. I could just sense something was not right. Then she would stand up straight, pull out the welfare money, and smile as she laid it on the counter.

That was about the time that I formed an awareness of money. Other families had some. We didn't.

By the time I hit age thirty, I felt rich. I went to Venezuela and Trinidad and Tobago. Met my future wife in Egypt. My life was full of road trips and dinners and gifts. I bought drinks for anyone who was around. In about two decades, I'd gone from food stamps to a seven-figure net worth. I thought that mattered. I felt different. I looked at myself differently, like I was part of a different club. I could do things my parents couldn't do. I had choices.

It wasn't hard for me to find new competitors to put up on the scoreboard. It was part of my everyday life as a salesperson. The sales world is full of ex-athletes because it is competitive by its very nature. The customer either buys from you or they don't. They go with your company or they go with a competitor. Win or lose. An entire culture is built around playing this sales game, keeping track of the score, and eventually keeping track of wins and losses.

Quotas are assigned and displayed for the entire company to see. Updates are displayed for the entire company to see. Whether Blue is on top or bottom, whether he is winning or losing, relative to quota or his peers, is on public display through spreadsheets or charts.

My managers pushed and pulled me much as my coaches did. One more call. One more meeting. Push a little harder. Give a little more, then give some more, and tomorrow we'll start at ground zero and hammer at it again and again.

Most of my sales career was spent with startups. These were young companies, most of which had no customers, just a product idea and millions in venture capital. Attempting to be the first to sell a new software solution, millions of untouchable bits and bytes, was extremely challenging. Especially when the price point was in the tens or hundreds of thousands of dollars.

A couple of the startups I was a part of ran low on seed money at some point. We were faced with either closing a deal, begging for more money from an investor, or having to make some tough decisions about who was going to get whatever money was left.

But the rewards were huge. The sales teams I was a part of were paid very well. Much of the compensation was on display. Extravagant trips for exceeding quota. Massive bonuses for closing big deals. Additional stock options for repeated success.

Besides the money, I found other ways to measure myself against others. I wanted the big title. "Sales rep" just wouldn't cut it anymore. Words like "senior" or "director" or "manager" mattered on my business card. In the late '90s, "options" were a big deal in Seattle. Little dot-com companies were sprouting up in every neighborhood in town. The executives would get significant salaries and hefty bonuses, along with a crazy number of stock options. The rest of us got decent salaries, sizable bonuses, and plenty of stock options. Tens of thousands of stock options for kids in their twenties with little to no experience.

A thousand options with one company, then a few thousand with the next, then eventually, after bouncing around in this playground full of dot-com ideas, tens of thousands of options. Thirty-five thousand options, at a seemingly very possible first-day closing price of thirty dollars each, equaled instant millionaire. "How many options did you get?" was a common question being asked in Seattle at the time.

My base salary, plus my potential bonus, plus my title, plus the number of stock options equaled my worth. Not my net worth. My self-worth.

My wife and I regularly discussed having a vacation home or second home while we were dating and through the early years of our marriage. Whenever we traveled, we would weigh the pros and cons of having a second home in that area. North or south? Mountains or lowlands? Ocean, lake, or river? Raw land then build or turnkey? Would we retire or vacation there? Is it better or worse than the last place we visited? Where might we be in ten or twenty years?

These discussions were a bit fantasy but rooted in reality. We were making enough money and had enough ambition that the conversations might actually become a reality. A few years after moving to Atlanta, we were back in Seattle for the holidays and ended up out in a farming valley about an hour north of the city. We drove past a sign that said "Land for Sale" and decided on a whim to check it out.

It was a big piece of land, five parcels totaling 175 acres, on just under a mile of riverfront. There was a one-hundred-year-old barn, a house, three ponds, and a tree farm with irrigation. Objectively, this was an interesting piece of property. The price seemed right. The volume of land was unique. Its location relative to Seattle was prime. The county had been growing like gangbusters since I started paying attention to real estate just out of college.

On an emotional level, the property was more than just interesting to me. I had always been fascinated by old barns, both outside of Roseburg and outside of Milton-Freewater. I loved rivers, having such fond memories of growing up with rope swings and skipping rocks and innertube floating. The size and flow of the river, and the relationship of the land to it, with its outward bend past all the trees, reminded me of where I grew up in Roseburg.

As importantly, I thought it would impress people if I had a bunch of land like that. Anyone could buy stocks and mutual funds, jewelry, and art. Sure, I could buy a cabin, but a bunch of people were doing that. Some I knew were buying bits of land here and there. But nobody I knew was moving on something like that.

We bought it, and I felt like I was king of the castle.

We had our first child a couple of months later. A boy. He was the easiest baby, on a sleeping and eating schedule within a few weeks. No fussing. Completely healthy.

I couldn't believe the love I felt. The speed at which I was completely enraptured by him blew me away. It couldn't have taken thirty minutes. All of a sudden, that was the most important thing in my life. I had no idea it could happen that fast. There was also a sense of pride. I pushed through my doubt and found the pot of gold.

After a few months of thoroughly enjoying this new piece to my family, I woke up one morning, went to my home office, sat down, and stared at the wall.

I have it all. An amazing wife that I couldn't even dream up. Great kid. A sweet house in a great neighborhood. A barn on a river. Too many friends to count, new and old. Retirement secured. Hell, I have even more than I ever could have imagined.

Now what? I have another fifty years of living ahead of me. Across every scoreboard I had created in my mind, I won. *What's next?*

I needed a new scoreboard.

I came up with a ranking system to measure how well I was doing as a person. Financially, I made up goals. At age twenty-two, I had a goal of earning twice my age. When I blew past that, I told myself four times my age meant I was successful. Then a million-dollar net worth. Then a million dollars in disposable assets. Those were the big goals. I always kept little goals around. Make more money than last quarter, more money than last year. Beat the market. It was constant.

I made up relationship goals. I didn't measure that goal in how many friends I had. I measured how good of a friend I was. Was I calling all of the people I cared about on a regular basis? Was I having beers or lunch with them? Was I supporting them? Asking about their lives? Wishing them a happy birthday?

The April after my dad took off for good, I forgot my mom's birthday. It was just my little brother and me to remember, and I didn't. No cake, no card, no presents. The day just slipped by. Eventually, just before bed, my mom broke down and started crying. She reminded me that it was her birthday and no one remembered. I was so embarrassed. I was shocked at myself for forgetting. I said I was sorry over and over, and my mom just comforted me. I told myself it would never happen again, but it didn't matter. I had to live with that. One day, I couldn't remember one day. I still feel that guilt every April. I multiplied that guilt whenever I found out about a friend's birthday after the fact.

But I never made a birthday calendar.

Since I was no longer in school, I couldn't measure the mental part of me through tests and grades, so I took IQ tests on the internet. I would challenge myself to online brain teasers. Could I get into Mensa?

My measurement of my physical self was easy. Not just run a 10K but run it as fast as I could. Then faster the next time. Find out what was "good" for someone my age and try to beat that. Bench press, then bench press more. Run a marathon, then a duathlon. Exercise five days a week. Then six. How many miles a week? What's my plan to do more next month?

I mixed my drinking achievement in with all of these goals. Have eight beers and three shots, then get up and run four miles. Go on a weekend road trip, drinking for thirty-two of the forty-eight hours, then bounce and work out all week.

That was how I was better than the rest. Others might be able to run a 5K faster than me, but I drank a fifth of Jack last week, and I still finished ahead of most. Could I close the deal after staying up partying until 3 a.m.? That was the true measure of the man. Everybody in my work world drank, and drank hard. The old work hard, play hard mentality. If you were good, really good, you could go past midnight getting drunk, then make your 7 a.m. meeting and close the deal. Winners stayed at the bar. Losers went home.

I also got to use drinking as a crutch. I didn't stop beating myself up for not achieving the expectations I set for myself. That was a given. But if I wanted to, I could use the drinking to lessen the pain. OK, it took over an hour to finish that 10K. I drank four nights last week. In that category, the category of thirty-year-olds who weighed two-hundred pounds and drank more than twenty drinks last week, I was still in the top quartile.

I was pretty good at making new scoreboards and tournament brackets.

There is an expectation from athletes to suck it up and play hurt. For me, this expectation came from the inside more than the outside. My competitive side wanted to push through the pain to beat the next guy to the finish line, or the ball, or the basket. To get up and do it again, one more time than the other guy. To take the best they could throw at me and hit it right back at them. To not lose. Those were the things that drove me.

Until the scoreboards that I conjured up stopped working. The go-go world I strived to be a part of stopped making sense.

While working for IBM, or walking between cubicles at clients such as Coca-Cola and Walmart, I wondered *what are all of these people doing here*? I knew, of course, that some people needed to be around to make the company run. But, so many of them? What are ALL of them doing here?

It was like a Dilbert cartoon. I didn't see human beings, just zombies moving aimlessly between meetings and break rooms, punching clocks as they meandered to and from.

As a competitive, ambitious sales guy peeking in from the outside, it seemed as if most people were just doing the bare minimum possible to keep their jobs. No one wanted to break the mold. Just maintain the status quo, maybe there will be less work to do, and you can get out of this place. I wondered, why are you even here? If you don't want to improve the company and improve your career, what are you doing?

I started looking at the software solutions I was selling, wondering what they were for. To help some Fortune 500 company squeak another half-percent of profit out of their billions in revenue? There were tens of thousands of people at the company doing ... what exactly? Not saving lives. Not improving the global water supply. Not helping a parent get back on her feet.

Everyone was chasing a buck, including me. I started to become cynical about business and virtually anything about making money. But I kept at it, sort of. I bounced from company to company, trying to keep my name on the scoreboard while questioning the entire game. I couldn't retire, but I was having trouble staying motivated. The need to have stuff just wasn't there anymore.

What else was I going to do, though? I was a salesperson. I made money for the company, and the company gave me plenty in return. That's all I was. What else was there?

At my in-laws' place, there was a bar to the left, just as you walked in the front door. An actual, legit bar that could have been downstairs at a speakeasy. There were places for every kind of drinking glass and separate sections for fifths, liqueurs, wine, mixers. Very cool bar-appropriate art and lighting. In one of the drawers was an old-school bartending manual.

Instructions on how to act like a bartender and a massive glossary full of recipes of every drink ever created.

At family gatherings, we would pull that bartending book out and pick random drinks to make. Just flip the pages, eyes closed, and point your finger down somewhere on one of the two pages. About everyone would have fun giving it a go, trying to follow the recipe as closely as possible, laughing at the absurdity of some combination. Those drinks could get pretty elaborate. Most of the time, we didn't have every ingredient of the drink, so the current mixologist would substitute whatever was in the house that might be close. As the night rolled on, most people would fade away from the bar, leaving only the regulars to keep mixing. Once the mixing crowd faded off to bed, only the real drinkers would still be awake, and we didn't concern ourselves with mixing.

One late night I found myself with a cousin a few years younger than me, just the two of us at the bar. He was a good drinker. Probably great. A formidable foe. We had beers and booze. Then more, and then another, continuing until I felt myself slipping. I was drunk, and it didn't seem he was. But I kept at it, even though something was off. I kept feeling drunker and drunker, and he kept looking stronger and stronger. *Goddammit, keep up!*

Eventually, I had to tap out. I could have kept going, but it would have been futile. He was going to outlast me.

And that was it. My time was up. I gave up and went to bed. The last thing I was any good at, I wasn't good at anymore.

CHAPTER 5

Depression

After leaving Atlanta, we moved into a house in Kirkland. Back in Kirkland, twenty-two years later. One afternoon, the irony of this dawned on me when we took the kids down to the playground at Houghton Beach Park, a five-minute drive from our house. It is a beautiful park, right on the lake, across the water from the University of Washington, with a few grassy areas, a small sandy beach, a dock, a playground, and a sand volleyball pit.

As I watched my kids on the play structure, I looked to my right. I realized that this was the same volleyball court I'd cut class to visit during my junior year in high school at Juanita. Sometimes with Todd, sometimes with Scott.

On the one hand, I felt fortunate to live so close to such a wonderful park. To be able to take my healthy and happy son and daughter to this place, just minutes away from my home, was like a dream scenario. To have made it full circle, back to a place where I had such fun, felt incredible to me.

Yet there was anguish that accompanied this town, and this place specifically. Scott and Todd were no longer with me. I was in the town where I had been forced to move, leaving behind my perfect childhood setting. It was the town in which my mom had contracted cancer. The great times in Kirkland were accompanied by such loss and pain.

I was baffled by the mix of emotions. I didn't know if I could go down to Houghton again. I told myself that was just silly talk. It was an amazing place. What a great place to include in my children's upbringing. What great memories they could make.

But what bad memories for me.

My mind started to meander. What had I done? How could I have allowed myself to buy a home so close to this place? What was I doing back in Kirkland? What was I doing to myself? Was I ready for this?

All of these questions hit me at regular intervals as I drove through and around my old stomping grounds. If we stayed in our current house, the kids would go to my rival high school. *Booooo*, I thought, followed by chuckles as I drove past it, even all these years later.

I remembered Scott telling me stories about crazy parties during Moss Bay Days as I drove past the Downtown Marina. I recalled bootlegging or using a fake ID to get alcohol at the Super 24 on Lake Washington Boulevard, or Market Street, or the one up on Finn Hill. Driving by the old apartments I thought of Mom, Uncle Tom, and the Juanita crew. Driving by the old Chevy dealership, I thought of my summer job. Passing Peter Kirk baseball field, I remembered my days with the Pepsi American Legion baseball team.

Old memories haunted me even as present-day experiences formed new memories in my head. New jogs along the lake. Eating at new restaurants. Newfound joy from watching my kids feed the ducks, or slide down the slide, or run really-super-fast in the grass, laughing all the way. My brain was overloaded with analysis and wondering. Confusion.

I couldn't comprehend it all. I couldn't make sense of the bliss and fun layered on top of grief and anger. How could this be? How was I supposed to feel? How can one person handle all of this? Why do I have to handle all of this? *Mom, where are you to help me answer these questions? Dammit, Mom!* I was bound and determined to keep going, to push on. It didn't matter about my recent failures or whether I was doing the right thing. Or whether I even needed to be doing whatever it was I thought I needed to be doing. I was going to plow through. I didn't feel like I was rushing through a time that needed to be slowed down. There was no time to consider what was happening to me. It was go-time. It was always go-time. Urgency and staying ahead of the clock were constants. I moved forward, the only direction I knew.

Before moving back, I talked to a few companies about job openings, narrowed it down to two, then flew out to Seattle for more intensive interviews. With former workmates at each company, I ended up with offers from both. Even though it didn't feel entirely right, I went with the company that offered more stock options and seemingly more freedom outside of work. I could tell that the culture wasn't a great fit, but my real desire at the time was to become a country man on the property we purchased north of Seattle in Snohomish County. A farmer. A blue-collar guy. Living off the land and raising my kids through the lessons of an honest day's work.

By this point, I had become disgusted with the corporate world. The excess and waste. The laziness and apathy. People making hundreds of thousands of dollars for … what? To sell another can of sugar water? To make another .001% on a loan? To pay for another employee-of-the-month to fly to Cabo first class?

I was going to earn my keep. Get back to reality. Put in a hard day's work on the land we had purchased. I started Trafton Trees to carry on the tree farm that ran on most of the 175 acres we bought. I had business cards made that showed a simple logo I made up. I established an LLC with the state of Washington. I came to a business arrangement with someone who was going to manage the day-to-day operations of the tree farm and bought a bunch of saplings and planted them. From there, I figured the business and the trees would just grow automatically.

I had visions of us being part of the real estate growth around Puget Sound, but as someone who was part of the construction, not the financing. I thought my whole family would get involved, that my kids, even though they would inherit a bunch of money, would learn from working the land.

But I couldn't do it immediately. I needed to live a double life for a while until I got established up at the farm. I took a job that my gut wasn't really comfortable with, the idea being that I could just wing it for a couple of years.

I had two kids, ages three and one, one of whom wasn't sleeping through the night yet, a wife who worked more than full time at a new job that required after-hours attention, a brand-new business I was trying to get off the ground, a new home, two rental properties, plus over 160 acres that needed maintaining.

While I'd been living in Atlanta, my brother and both of my wife's brothers had two kids each as well. Four nieces and two nephews in Seattle. In-laws, aunts, an uncle, a cousin. All to see and do stuff with. I felt an obligation to all of them.

But what I really felt was, I Was Back, Baby! Ready to party with the fellas that I hadn't hung out with in six years. Thursday beers and Saturday clubs. Live music and happy hours. Cookouts and ball games.

I was going to do it all!

I pushed myself even harder. Waking up in the middle of the night to work on the tree farm. Pulling double duty during the day, making calls for both companies, scheduling a meeting for one outfit based on a commitment with another outfit. I would stay up late drinking, then wake up in the wee hours to take care of the kids. I would see family on my way to see buddies. Kept drinking like I did when the only responsibility I had was me.

As I pushed my life ahead, my mind started to push back. Something about my Self wasn't right, and my vision became blurry. Not literally, as in my eyesight. Figuratively, as in unable to comprehend reality. What I wanted wasn't really a possibility. No way all of it was going to work out. My answer was to turn down the volume of my inner voice, which was telling me I couldn't do it all. I just saw the scoreboard. Everyone and everything became the opposition. No one could tell me otherwise. I had to have more, get more, be more. Being tired was a sign of weakness. Doing less was giving up. There was no endgame, no finish line.

I demanded that I have the freedom of a fifteen-year-old, the energy of a twenty-five-year-old, and the sensibilities of a thirty-five-year-old. Simultaneously, every day.

I knew I had to stop drinking, as well as make other changes. I knew that my paying job wasn't working out and that my dream job wasn't going anywhere. I was becoming short with my wife. I couldn't stop drinking, though. I couldn't stop trying to do it all, either. I couldn't tell other people that

I had to give up on my tree farm. Or that I couldn't go out that night. Or that I wasn't going to drink. Or that I wasn't working out six days a week. I couldn't let people know that I couldn't handle it all.

I didn't tell anyone about my internal struggles either. Not even my wife.

On the surface, everything looked great. I had a nice house in a nice neighborhood. Healthy kids in a great school district. An amazing wife. And I could be whoever I needed to be. A well-to-do startup technology businessman, a blue-collar, gritty, country-music-loving farmer, and a Superdad.

My lowest priority at the time was my actual paying job. I was a salesman working remotely out of my home. My only job was to sell. No one cared when I worked or how much I worked. Just that I was hitting my quota. I took advantage of that. I didn't care, sincerely care, about making more money or selling anything. All I felt I needed to tell people was that I had this cool job working for a technology startup and plenty of stock options that would pay off when the company exited.

In my head, the only purpose of my real job was to facilitate my other job. The purpose of my other job was to live out an image of the person I thought I should be, which meant any life other than those I had experienced. Those corporate guys could have their midlevel management, chain-restaurant, suburban lives. Those Richie-Rich's could wear their fancy clothes and drive their fancy cars. I just wanted to be something else. Whatever I was doing, I just wanted to be doing something else.

I would head out for an evening with the fellas knowing full well that I couldn't handle the drinking. I knew I would be up at 3 a.m. with my daughter, then 7 a.m. with my son. Every day of the week. Neither of my kids had learned about weekends yet. But I couldn't give up the partying. I couldn't give up trying to succeed at that even though every night ended in failure.

I also wanted to be a good husband, but that, too, was slipping. As the pressures mounted and each piece of my life failed to live up to my expectations, the stress rose to the surface. I had to act cool around everyone outside my home, and I couldn't take it out on my kids, so my wife began to get the burden of my craziness. Everything she said was wrong. Everything I thought was right. Her ideas were stupid. Mine were great. She didn't know. I knew. I knew it all.

Within a year of moving back to Seattle, I was losing it.

I got fired from my job, but I told myself that was what I wanted anyway. That job was just getting in the way of life I thought I wanted to make. I had such disdain for the life I was living, and I looked down on just about every other type of life around me. Suburbs or city. Big company or little company. Rich or middle class. High tech or low tech. Whatever environment I was in was a perception that I wanted no part of. I became anti-everything. Everything was dumb except me.

I was awesome. But I was accomplishing nothing. I sucked.

I was still telling myself I could do it all. I found another job that I thought would give me the freedom to do it all, but it was a huge pay cut. I was losing sight of the fundamental purpose of working, to get paid. I just kept working because I was supposed to keep working.

Working no longer was paying off. Drinking was no longer paying off.

About three months into the new job, I was driving down Interstate 5 to go to work and started bawling like a baby. I didn't want this life. I was making no money, becoming less healthy by the day, and had no hope for the tree business. I didn't want to party anymore, but I didn't know how to stop. Barely maintaining the speed limit, trying to see through the tears in my eyes, I called my Aunt Kay.

I blabbered for a bit until she said, "Oh honey, you're depressed."

My eyes cleared up and my mind went blank. Depressed. It just couldn't be. There was no way Blue Andrews, with my amazing life, could be depressed. *Come on*, I thought. *No Way.*

Silence. But I had stopped crying.

She said it again. "You're depressed."

My only response was, "What?"

She told me I needed to talk to a professional. That a lot was going on inside me. That I was lost. She said all of this so gently, with great compassion, no judgment. It didn't feel harsh. It felt like the truth. My aunt became the all-seeing wise one. She described all of the symptoms of depression I was showing, and I couldn't disagree with one. There was so much about me that I knew to be true but just couldn't accept.

I told her I wasn't depressed, just tired. I made excuses about kids and jobs.

She talked me through my drive until I pulled into the parking lot at work. I wiped away the tears, put on one of my happy songs, Pat Green's "Carry On," and got myself together. Then I headed into work, acting normal, just another day.

The conversation with my aunt pulled back just a tiny piece of the façade I had been hiding behind, exposing something that I was feeling but could not see. I knew there was more to explore, more to understand, which would be scary. I set it aside, didn't tell anyone, didn't discuss it further with my aunt.

The only person I wanted to lead me back was my mom. "I just want my mom," would spill out of my mouth, and I would shake my head as I expressed this feeling. I knew it made no sense, coming from a grown man. But those were the words I felt.

I wouldn't know how to parent and would start sobbing, "I just want my mom." If anything went wrong during the day, even the slightest of transgressions, whether from someone known or a complete stranger, my head started spinning, and I wouldn't be able to function. I fell and fell until the only thing I wanted was my mom.

As my depression grew, I sank further and further into my youth, causing me to respond to the everyday circumstances of the world like a teenager. More than once, after a hard night of drinking, I would strip off all my clothes, go find an empty bed in the house, and curl up in the fetal position. I would cry and long for my mom to hold me. I knew that, emotionally, I had become a toddler. Yet I couldn't keep myself from going there.

One evening I arrived home from work on edge. From everything. My job. My small business. My property. My family. My body. Every stressor was bubbling just below the surface. The kids weren't home, so I poured myself a few more fingers of bourbon than normal, no ice, and assumed a position that had become more and more frequent. I sat down in the leather chair in the TV room and just stared down at a spot on the rug about six feet in front of me. Dazed. All the internal arguments just became white noise between my ears.

My wife got home not long after that. She tried to start a normal conversation, but I would have none of it. I knew she sensed the state I was in and understood something was very off. Still, I imagine she was also like me, unable to define what exactly was going on. She finally commented that something was wrong, and I exploded. Sandy went into the other room. I took off without saying a word, without my phone.

When I left my house, I drove to look for my mom. I was well on my way to drunk, having polished off a couple of extra-large pours of whiskey by that point. That meant I needed more to drink. I stopped off at a mini-mart and grabbed a few small bottles of wine to drink in my car as I began this journey that had entered my mind many times before.

I drove to the apartment complex in Totem Lake that I lived in when my mom died. Even by this point in the early evening, with the sun still out, I wasn't seeing straight. With tears in my eyes and booze in my veins, I found the parking lots and buildings that housed my former home. I'd driven past it a few times during the last few years but never ventured in. Though it was twenty years later, I was determined to find my way to the exact apartment we'd lived in.

I weaved around and by and back around various buildings for a while until I spotted the row of buildings I thought was ours. I knew it was toward the back, butting up against a wetland that I walked through to get to high school. I parked at one end and walked around back searching.

Even though I was basically walking through a bunch of other people's backyards, I didn't notice a thing. My blinders were on. I just wanted to stand behind my old apartment. I wanted to look out into the trees, beyond the pond, to see what my mom would have seen. I just wanted to get as close as physically possible to the life that once included a mom.

I sensed that the families who lived in the apartments near where I was standing were watching me, but I didn't care. This was my pursuit. I had bottled up so much angst that it was of no consequence that I was intruding on someone else's life now. I cried, barely able to see through the tears but peering intently into the sky, waiting for my mom to show.

I stood back there for what felt like hours. Long enough that it was now becoming dusk. But my mom never showed. I asked, "Why? Why? Why did you go? Why won't you come back?"

I got back in the car and continued my journey into the beyond by looking for Scott and Nancy Hardie. I knew that would hurt too, and maybe in different and worse ways. I knew that I was just digging myself deeper into the disorder. Something was telling me I had to do it. I had to walk on these coals.

I didn't care that I was driving drunk. I didn't care about hurting myself anymore. I didn't care that what I was doing was insane. I was Alice, and I was diving headfirst into the rabbit hole.

I drank more wine on the drive from Totem Lake up to Kingsgate as the sun set further. I laughed, thinking about how lost I was about to become, just as lost as I had been twenty years earlier trying to find the first party Scott had invited me to. I knew it wouldn't be easy to find the Hardie house with the roads that seemed to all wind back into each other. But I had a couple more bottles of wine and all the time in the world. There was nothing in my life I had to get back to.

I finally found Scott's old house. The one I spent the night in. The one that I ate dinners at. The one that I completed school projects in. The one in which an entire family happily lived. I drove by it, turned around, drove by it again, turned around, and then pulled up and stopped across the street from it. The dunk hoop. The split level. The little manicured yard out front. Now that was a home. Except now, everyone was gone.

I took my last bit of wine and attempted to find one of the parks in this perfectly designed suburban neighborhood. I was seventeen again, just trying to find some friends to hang out with. I stumbled upon a park, got out, walked to the little play area with my wine, and sat in the swing. I pictured the high school girls doing the same thing, with the boys showing off on the grass. I just wanted everything back to the way it was. Denim jackets lined with fake fur. An ABC or Psychedelic Furs or Beastie Boys cassette in the boombox. Stroh's fifteen packs and 20/20 wine coolers stashed in the bushes with only playing sports and making out to worry about.

Next, I decided to try and find the rental I was living in with Scott when he got cancer. That one would be a bit tougher, but I found it anyway. I went back to the old Pizza Bank Italian restaurant, which I thought was so lavish at the age of sixteen, and worked my way from that landmark. I pulled across from the dark wood ranch-style home and just shook my head. How could that have all happened? How could our high school dream of living together after college come true and then be destroyed, all within a couple of years?

Why did they all have to die!?

I remembered a couple of the bars that were nearby. The ones that only I used to enjoy. Dives and cheesy pickup bars where people were there to forget whatever they left outside. Places that most twenty-somethings wouldn't venture into. The alcohol had worked its way through my system by this point, and I was full-on drunk. I was driving on instinct, stumbling into bars and ordering out of habit.

I was so self-conscious. I thought everyone was staring at me, just knowing the fool's errand I was in the middle of running. I knew what I was doing was crazy, so I figured it was written all over my person. But nobody said a word. They served me my drinks and took my money. One bar. Then another bar. Then another bar.

It was getting late, and I had gone from disoriented drunk to aware drunk. I needed to get back home. I didn't have my phone on me, and I figured Sandy would be wondering what was going on. I knew I hurt her when I initially noticed I hadn't taken my phone with me earlier in the night. I looked around the car, didn't see my phone, and made the conscious decision to continue on my trip anyway. She knew I was on edge and that I had started drinking in the early evening, which meant lots more drinking throughout the night.

Throughout the evening, it had gotten so bad for Sandy that she had to call in reinforcements. When I got home, my brother was there waiting for me. So was Steve Hardie, Scott's little brother, Nancy's son, who I now thought of as family, another brother. I was hammered, not really comprehending what they were saying. My brother was pissed off. What the hell were you doing? he asked. What the hell were you think-ing? he yelled. We walked around and around the swimming pool, me trying to avoid him and he not letting me slide off easily. I didn't have anything to say to him. I was embarrassed, sad, and disgusted with myself. So angry that I still wanted my mom after all these years. Even more angry I couldn't find her.

I was also pissed at him. *How could he not understand? Why isn't he right there beside me? Didn't he miss Mom too?* I couldn't talk to him. I didn't know what to say. How could I explain myself? He threw his hands up at me and left.

Steve, on the other hand, was a little lighter on me. He just wondered what I was doing. It was easier to talk with him. I told him I had gone out searching for my mom and his mom and his brother. He just laughed and said, "What the hell did you do that for? I can't even do that." I shook my head and laughed as well. From the moment I hopped in the car that evening, I knew what I was getting myself into, and I went for it anyway. We sat in silence for a little while. I caught my breath, and he sensed I had settled down. "You good?" he asked. I nodded my head. We stood up, hugged, and he took off.

The next morning I finally admitted out loud, to myself and Sandy, that something was seriously wrong. The night before was scary, but it was also a sign. I needed help. Sandy pushed it, and I didn't argue. This had gone beyond missing someone. Or being sad. Or grieving. I was no longer feeling depressed. I was now in Depression. With a capital D. The actual sickness. *I have Depression.*

In between Depression and grieving sits depression with a small d. Not quite a disease, but more than a bad day. No loss to point at. No "real" reason for feeling down, but it's there. A funk. A little bit off. Something akin to having the flu and getting dumped by your girlfriend on the same weekend. It lasts for a while. More than a week. Less than six months. Just a general "ugh."

Of course, I am no doctor. This is just my perception of the phases of anguish I went through during adulthood, me trying to make sense of so much that didn't make sense. I found comfort in attaching my own labels to my feelings.

Feeling depressed manifested itself in general apathy toward everything. I didn't have an interest in seeing people or talking with anyone. Goals? Meh. Accomplishing something? Whatever. Should I do what I'm supposed to do? Don't care. I exercised, but not all out. Got my chores done, but maybe only partially. Just enough that the house still functioned. Instead of opportunities to be of service, I saw them as obligations that must be met. Other people, society in general, seemed indifferent as well.

When it was merely depression with a small d, I could get out of bed just fine. I usually had enough energy in the morning, maybe even had a positive attitude for a few hours. But by midafternoon, I was zapped. My mind started to swirl around, unable to land on any single thought for more than a few seconds. My patience level waned when my head took over. Smiling and kindness were forced. It was just so draining to function positively in the world.

The most significant difference between feeling depressed and having Depression is duration and intensity. In the former, I may spend a few minutes getting myself up and at 'em, then be fine the next day. The latter puts me in that state for hours at a time every day. Frustration and a range of other emotions set in, which exacerbated the situation. More emotions just meant more energy to manage them.

In my personal experience and observation—no scientific research involved—I estimate the duration for depression to be in the few weeks range. Sometimes just a few days. Depression, the big one, is feeling depressed for six months to maybe a year at least. It just doesn't go away until you're adrift in the water with no harbor anywhere on the radar.

Picture a father with his three-year-old daughter and an afternoon with no plans. It's wet and cold outside, so they decide to head to the mall. They play on those quarter arcade rides, get ice cream, maybe pick up a fun gift for Mom. There's no rush, plenty of time to just be together. At one of the big department stores, something catches the daughter's eye—a stuffed animal as big as she is. They venture in and start meandering through the aisles and racks.

"Look at this HUGE unicorn, Daddy."

They talk about her favorite toy. Then, what if she was a princess and the unicorn was her pet? Just a wonderful conversation.

Then something catches dad's eye. A craft for his wife that she could make with their daughter. He grabs his daughter's hand, and they go in for a closer inspection. He lets go of her hand to pick it up. Inspect it. Then grabs a different variety of craft, then another. Various sizes and colors, different levels of difficulty. All the while, he's picturing his wife and daughter laughing, spending quality time together. Then he envisions the three of them on the couch, admiring the new art they created together. He could put it up in his office, he thinks.

He looks down and asks, "Hey sweetie, what do you think?"

Except she's not there. Where could she be? He walks around a bit, calling her name. Fifteen seconds go by. His voice picks up volume. Another fifteen seconds of walking and calling. Except now it feels like ten minutes. The calling turns to yelling. "I've lost my daughter. HELP!" Another minute goes by, except now it feels like an hour. Yelling! Others catch on and start looking. The scene becomes frantic. The father is now sweating. He is picturing a white van, needles, and duct tape. Then a cargo van full of other little girls headed for a boat at some West Coast inlet.

At the same time, the little girl is sobbing. She is wandering around, lost, unable to see Daddy. She walks up to legs that are wearing pants just like her daddy's. Except none of them are Daddy. She is crying. Completely lost. The most scared she's ever been. She freezes, eyes as wide as the moon, unable to speak.

Being sick with the disease called Depression felt like a combination of both the father's and the daughter's emotional state.

Like the father, aware enough to know that something awful was going on but feeling helpless to stop it. Visualizing just how messed up life was but unable to prevent the train from teetering off the rails. Picturing the absolute worst possible scenario.

At the same time, like the little girl. Every possible comfort is the wrong one. Nonstop questioning and confusion. Lost. Afraid. No idea what to do next. No idea what is really happening.

This is what my Depression was like.

Having Depression meant that feeling depressed had now moved beyond just my gut and heart, and into my arms and legs. Having Depression immobilized me with uncontrollable crying, confusion, and helplessness. It was scary and cruel, taking over my mind.

During some moment of coherent thinking, when the disease wasn't completely in control, I recognized that it was time for professional help. It probably meant drugs, definitely some serious focus.

Once I acknowledged I had Depression and my wife jumped on board with me, we considered treatment. What was I supposed to do? How does this get "fixed"? What was really wrong with me?

One thing we knew was that a bunch of people close to me had died. It was likely that I hadn't adequately dealt with that. Plus, I was longing for my mom, the extent of which only I knew. Since it happened in my youth, we went to a very close family friend, an expert on loss and grieving in young people. She connected me with a therapist specializing in young people who lost a parent.

I didn't feel like this was perfect, but I also didn't know what was perfect, or what was even close to being the best thing to do. I sure felt like a teenager, highly emotional, still, over my mom and dad. It seemed as good a start as any. After a few weekly sessions, I didn't feel my head or heart feeling any deep connection to any part of the therapy.

I continued my search for help, which I was OK with. I recognized that this Depression had been building up inside me for years and that it would likely take years to go away. Since I was confused, how was I to give guidance on the help I needed? That was my thinking.

Concurrent to this, we thought it might be prudent to look into antidepressant drugs. My primary care physician recommended a psychiatrist, Dr. Martini. The irony of his name alone should have been enough for me to look elsewhere. But I just went with it. After all, my doctor was with the world-renowned University of Washington Medical Center.

After providing about forty minutes of fairly superficial and basic information, the doctor prescribed drugs, an antidepressant. I didn't ask questions or seek another opinion. All I knew was that I needed help. I just started taking the drugs.

I also stopped drinking, but only for about six weeks. Then I continued with the antidepressants while going back to consuming a depressant. In measured amounts at first, but eventually back to the heavy drinking that I'd been doing before "That Night."

I saw Dr. Martini a few more times, but he wasn't doing much for me. Every session, he would ask variations of the same, basic, seemingly generic questions. Then he would write me another prescription. *Did it even matter how I answered?*

After a short while, I stopped seeing him and just went back to the UW clinic for my prescription. Something felt odd about that, though, too. Here was this general practitioner, who was seeing people of all ages, for every kind of malady possible, for about twenty minutes at a time. She was the one prescribing mind-altering drugs to me?

Both doctors described the drugs as "mild" antidepressants. That didn't click either. I felt like what I had clearly wasn't mild. I was really messed up inside. This wasn't just some bit of sadness over a chick that dumped me. I knew I was seriously messed up. Plus, I knew I could handle my drugs. Give me the super-dose.

What good was this doing? I attempted to do my own research, finding my own path. But I couldn't find a standard, tried-and-true solution for Depression either. I just stuck with a random prescription at the recommended dose.

We tried another psychiatrist who played the part a little better than the first. In his dark-wood office with a leather couch wearing corduroy trousers and a cardigan, he spoke like a professor. He offered me a new antidepressant. Again, I didn't pay much attention to the name or the dose. I just took my piece of paper to a drugstore, had it filled, and followed orders. Though none of it felt right, nothing felt right. It was all so much work.

I started seeing another counselor. This guy was billed as a specialist in middle-aged men with drinking problems. He came across as kind of a guy's guy, a little rough and weathered. Language not as polished as Mr. Psychiatry Professor.

His office was close to my house.

We discussed many topics concerning the past, present, and future. Loss, dad, wife, family, drinking, career, goals. I couldn't quite figure out what direction or style this guy was taking. I wasn't sure that we were on the same page, but I knew I needed to be telling someone something about me. Anything would be better than where I was. I went back, week after week, going through the ups and downs of recovery. Good day, bad day. Progress, confusion.

One day he said to me, "You know, there's nothing unique about you."

Well, that sure flexed my muscles. I sat straight up. *What the hell are you talking about? I'm me, and I'm awesome.* But I didn't say anything. Didn't want to rock the boat.

A few days later, after stewing over it constantly, I figured that I would give him the benefit of the doubt. I assumed he was saying that I wasn't the only one out there with problems, even my specific problems. People overcome them. There are strategies and methods for overcoming this. This ain't the world's first Rodeo of the Downtrodden. *Deep breaths. You got work to do.*

However, I couldn't let that statement go. Even after a few more sessions, those words continued to stick with me. *For a person who has Depression, who thinks they are a piece of shit, who thinks life isn't worth living, I wonder if letting them know they aren't special is really the right approach?*

We continued along at a flat pace. I was neither really feeling great about this guy nor feeling like I was going back down to my dark place either. I continued to read up on him, trying to understand whether I was doing the right thing, and found that he was also a specialist in sexual issues. Not sure exactly what that meant, but I thought I'd try him out. I told him about the time I found my parents naked in their bedroom. Something was happening, sexually, that didn't look right. I was about ten.

Well, that got him to sit up in his chair a little bit. He wanted to talk all about it. *I have alcohol and Depression issues, and you want to talk about my mom and dad's sex life?* I stopped seeing him after the next session.

I was still trying to act as if nothing was wrong. I went to work with determination and urgency. I met with clients with all the feel-good I could muster. Smiled at strangers. Participated in social events with both family and friends. Tried to be a good husband and a great parent.

The Depression was not subsiding. It got to be most days, not just some days, that I used massive amounts of energy just to get out of bed and get going for the day.

Just get out of bed. Get out of bed, Blue! Get out of bed! Then it was, *just get out of the shower. Turn the handle and grab the towel.*

Man, I did not want to get out of the shower. By then, I was awake, and I knew what the day had in store. Pain. Grief. Sadness. Anger. Frustration. It would require more energy than I had left in the tank. Negativity grew, and grew, and grew. I would hold back the tears and shut off the shower.

Then it was into the closet and more coaxing. *OK, just put one arm in the sleeve. One arm. Get your clothes on.* The drive to work was awful, full of dread of the day ahead. Knowing the effort it would take to talk to people, to act normal. My car became a sweatbox.

Once out of my car, I thought everyone could see right through me. I thought they would see the Depression and every form of emotion it generated. This may have been because I saw right through them. Not to their internal thoughts. Beyond them. No one was there. It was just blurry, moving stuff. It was all just stuff.

Such a worldview eventually became the way I felt about myself. I was no longer there. No one cared about me. No one really liked me. Other people were more important. If I didn't show up one day, it wouldn't matter. Life would go on. The world would keep evolving. Business would get transacted. Games would still be played. Beer would still be swallowed.

This concept migrated to acquaintances, then to friends, then to family. Eventually, I didn't believe that anyone really cared about me. I had been nonexistent out in the world and now was nonexistent in my own house.

That was the final step into the abyss. Suicidal thoughts became familiar. I knew that I couldn't go on like this. Fighting every step of the way. Clearing one hurdle just to have four more come into view. Trying to function with the weight of a knight's armor draped on me at all times. I was in a never-ending steeplechase.

It was at this point I began to visualize a world without me.

I started thinking about life, the actual living part of life, in my twenties. That transitioned to contemplating the meaning of a person's life. Not life in general, just one life. Does it matter when someone's ends? The earth would still spin. The seasons would change. People would still get up and get into rush hour and sit in their cubicles. Stuff would get made and bought. I even considered those huge lives, like The President or The CEO or The Quarterback. If Bill Clinton wasn't around, there still would have been a U.S. president. The stock market, housing market, Germany, Disneyland—all would still hum along. Even inventors, like Edison or Ford. What if they weren't around? What if there was no refrigeration or computers or phones? Life would still go on. People lived for centuries without microwave ovens or golf clubs. If one person never existed, would it really matter?

Likely the thoughts of twenty-somethings since the beginning of time, they took on more meaning for me as I watched lives leave me.

In the end, I concluded that one life really didn't matter. In the whole scheme of things, philosophically speaking, any one single random life didn't matter. Then I concluded my life didn't matter. I was unimportant. Eventually, the conclusion was: I am useless.

I would let that line of thinking go for a while. Sometimes for hours. Sometimes briefly, sometimes daily. Sometimes I could go a week without thinking about it. Not dismissing it, but not focusing on it either. It would visit me from time to time when life got tough.

The "one life doesn't matter" philosophy coupled with the "everyone left me" idea started to sink in. I paired them up. They became one conclusion. I would contemplate those coupled ideas with a glass of whiskey, then resolve them as truth when I was sober. Or vice versa. Or when angry. Or frustrated. Or confident. By my late thirties, they had become foundational to my being.

My son was four and my daughter two. They would never remember me anyway. My wife was strong, smart, and driven. She had a large and amazingly supportive family. She would be fine. It was decision time. I needed to take drastic action about my situation before my son's fifth birthday, the time of my first memory, which was coming up on the calendar.

CHAPTER 6

Attempt

I felt like a ghost. As if no one could see me, my body nonexistent, thinking someone could just brush my shoulder and not feel a thing. People were talking through me, not to me. I was in the middle of a group of people who loved me, who were celebrating life. In my head, though, I was already gone.

Every year, a big family from Sandy's mom's side gets together in August for summer birthdays. They were scattered across the country, so the location of the shindig varied from year to year. This year, 2010, the celebration would take place in Seattle. There was a relative gravitational pull there, given that two of the kids were living in the same town.

These were people I loved and loved being around. Godmothers, international travel partners, and drinking buddies. The family I got to choose.

A couple of the guys were out on the back deck grilling. A couple of the gals were prepping in the kitchen. Another provided her usual contribution of cheering everything up— food, people, décor—with the touches of color and energy that she uniquely conveyed. Laughter filled the open spaces, and hugs took place around every corner.

The problem was, I couldn't participate. Not wouldn't. Couldn't. I could only observe conversations, not take part.

I felt incapable of uncontrollable laughter, unable to affectionately hug.

Over the years, being in sales and being a generally sociable guy, I'd become comfortable entering an existing conversation. I'd gently put my hand on the shoulder of someone in the group. Stick my head into the circle, only my head, pushing my neck out as far as it could, making a happy face. Start nodding and say, "Umhmmm, uh-huh," in a slightly but not too annoying manner. Look everyone in the eye until they made eye contact with me. Sometimes I could get a laugh. At least I would be allowed in.

On this night, none of that was happening. Instead, I looked for ways to stay in back of the action. I busied myself with party-preparation types of activities. I checked in on the kids more than normal. Engaging with the kids was always a great way to avoid real conversations with adults. I acted like I needed something in the car or had to take a call outside. I admired the furniture or the artwork or the trees. Anything but engage.

I had it in my head that the party was for them, not me. This was their family, Sandy's family, not mine. I was just a burden, a side note. I was invited out of politeness. The conversations about life weren't mine. The stories about work or hobbies weren't mine. The memories—of cousins growing up together, or past family birthday parties, or parents when they were younger—weren't mine.

Prior to hitting this party, I had given myself an out. A work colleague played in a band. They had a gig later that night at The Merchant Cafe in Pioneer Square, a touristy but still worthy historic district in downtown Seattle. Everyone at the family party knew how much I loved live music. They would all understand why I was leaving.

At the point I could pretend no longer, I let Sandy know I was taking off. She looked at me funny when I left, a combination of not understanding and anger, I felt, but she didn't push hard for me to stay either. Maybe she, too, was tired of the struggle. When I jumped in the cab, there was the slightest pull of guilt, but my ability to empathize was so close to zero by this point, so I didn't hesitate long. A passing thought wondering what I was doing leaving all these people lasted all of about three seconds.

I don't recall thinking specifically that I was about to hurt myself, but I also was prepared to do it if I felt like it. I'd been seeing and thinking about death for so long by that point. I'd weighed the plusses and minuses of staying alive for forty more years and how that would impact my friends and family. The scales had tipped pretty far away from living.

At The Merchant, it was tequila shots and beer. Every person I knew who walked through the door got one, which meant I got many. I was so excited to be out on the town, by myself, on a Friday night. To listen to live music. To know a member of the band. To hang out with some work buddies who I thought were pretty cool. I was trying to pump myself up. This was my element. This setting, full of trivial drinking buddies I hadn't met yet, this I could handle. Shots and beer. Shots and beer.

Toward midnight, after the band was offstage, a big group decided a change of venue was needed. I hopped into my boss's BMW 3 Series, and we headed to Fremont, a younger, hipper neighborhood bordering Lake Union. I got out of the car and stumbled into The Triangle. I was completely wasted, so I had just one beer at this stop. *Holy crap, I can barely see straight.* Now that I was with my boss, not just peers, I began to wonder what I was doing.

I walked outside for some fresh air, and my boss came up to me. We chitchatted on the personal side a bit. Then he shifted the conversation to manager stuff. Floating topics such as transitioning from a startup to a legitimate business. Closing bigger deals. Structuring the organization. Yep, or uh-huh, or right was the best I could muster in response to everything that came out of his mouth. Just nodded and tried to stand up straight, saying as little as possible, hoping not to slur too much. All I was hearing was blah, blah, blah … until the final few words.

"You're not A Closer," my boss said.

That's the worst thing anyone can say to a salesperson. Absolutely the worst. If it comes from your boss, it is twice as harsh.

I looked him in the eye. He stared straight back. I had nothing to say back to him. He was right. We both knew it. I took a big sip from my pint, set it down, and told my boss I had to go.

My body hopped in a cab, and I got in my head.

My boss nailed it. I'd been fired, effectively, from my last job. I had been the worst sales guy in my company before that. I was in the bottom half of producers at that very moment and wasn't showing any signs of moving up. I was a failure. I couldn't make money anymore. Neither could I think or create. I wasn't an athlete anymore. I was weak and slow, fat and drunk. My extended family didn't really care about me. My friends could take me or leave me. What did I have? Nothing.

I texted my wife, letting her know I was in a cab on my way home, even though I knew she was asleep. Covering my tracks. I got dropped off in our driveway, just in front of the garage doors. I always came in through the garage after a night of drinking, so that wouldn't be a surprise to my wife.

This time, though, instead of heading for the door that led inside the house, I headed to the workbench. Straight to the toolbox and the fresh pack of razor blades that I knew were there. Clean and ready for use.

One of my favorite movies was *The Big Chill*, a story about a group of old college friends who get together following the death-by-suicide of one of their old crew. Kevin Costner's stitched-up wrists are exposed briefly in the opening scene, just before the shirt cuffs are pulled over them and the procession of friends arriving at the funeral begins. I vividly remembered seeing the stitches over multiple straight-line scars.

As an eighth-grader, I pricked myself for a blood test in science class. I discovered that once I made the initial stab into my skin, the fear went away and I could poke through the skin over and over without much pain. So I did it, mostly to impress my football buddies and get the girls a little squeamish.

I made it out of the garage and shut the door. Sandy was a heavy sleeper so I figured there was a pretty good chance she wouldn't hear the garage door again. Nor would she stay awake long enough to realize I hadn't made it into bed.

Next to the house was a swimming pool and on the other side was a pool house. Inside was a shower. I walked in and sat on the floor of the shower. I figured this would make it easier to clean up. I pulled out a razor blade and started slicing my wrists, up and down along the vein, not sideways, to let more blood out. Like the wrists in the movie. After more than a dozen tequila shots and at least as many Bud Lights, there was no hesitation. For years I'd known I could cut myself.

I cut, and the bleeding started, but not as much as expected. Or hoped. It was dark, but I wasn't about to turn the light on in the pool house, in case Sandy was to look around for me. I moved the cutting over, sightly, less than an inch, to find a vein that might be a better bleeder. Then I cut deeper. Then cut longer. Then shifted over a millimeter or two and started cutting again.

After a few minutes, I knew I was bleeding because I could feel the stickiness of the blood as it dripped down my arm. It was getting on my pants and forming a little puddle that my hand stuck in. It was warm. Thicker than I had imagined and smelled somewhat salty. The rest of my clothes were getting wet and sticky too.

But I wasn't dying.

I didn't know what I should be expecting at that point. I hadn't gotten that far in my visions. But I thought I'd start to feel something. Something like what they talk about in the movies. Getting cold. Eyesight getting blurry. Losing consciousness. But I was actually gaining consciousness because the alcohol effect was starting to wear off. I was bleeding but wasn't dying.

I switched to the other arm. Cut. Cut. Cut. I was using my weak hand on my strong wrist, so I didn't feel as if I could be as accurate. I felt more blood, but still not enough. I couldn't feel death. I started squeezing my wrists, putting pressure at my elbow, then pushing down toward my hand, trying to force blood to come out. It wasn't working.

I needed to get the blood pumping.

I left the pool house and walked around the pool to the shed, where there were a few leftover landscaping paver stones and bricks. I grabbed one brick for each hand and started curling and pressing them over my head, getting my heart rate up so that more blood would pump out of the veins I'd opened up. After a few sets, I started walking, continuing with the curls and presses. *Shit, I am still alive.*

I got out to the main road and became aware that I was a drunk, bloody man walking around after 2 a.m. This was a nice part of town. Whenever there were headlights, I would jump into the darkness, behind a tree or bush. Then a bus passed. I knew more would be coming. *What if I just "fell" in front of one?* I heard another, but I couldn't do it. *Why can't I do this?* It would be great, maybe the ending I needed. With all my blood loss, just a slight hit would surely kill me, right? But I couldn't do it. There was some fear of the pain that I might briefly feel, some fear of failure. And thoughts that the driver or the riders might get hurt. I jumped back into the darkness as the next bus passed.

I walked by an office park with two- and three-story buildings and thought I should just jump off the roof. I made my way around a couple of them and couldn't see an easy way to get all the way up to the roof.

The lake was just down the hill. I knew a secluded area on the edge of Yarrow Bay where I figured I could just drown myself. I stood at the edge of a short dock. It was dark and secluded. I knew no one ever went down there because it was right next to the apartment complex we stayed at when we initially moved from Atlanta. I tried to figure out how I was going to pull this off. *The body fights death, doesn't it?* Maybe I could lie face down in the shallow water and then just put a bunch of rocks on my back, then push off and sink to the bottom. But Lake Washington water is really cold, even in August. And I was starting to feel a little cold myself. *Nope.* Couldn't do it.

I was out of options. My plan wasn't working. I walked down the road a bit, then up a hill to this other office complex hidden back in the trees. I wasn't going to even attempt climbing up to a roof at this point. Seemed futile. I was starting to realize I wasn't going to die. I couldn't kill myself, which was an incredibly awful feeling. Just completely demoralizing. Nothing was working out. There was nothing in my head that could make suicide a reality.

I meandered up the hill until I saw a grassy opening. There was a wooden picnic table, the kind you find in public parks, with the bench seats attached. Looked like this was where the smokers came on breaks. It was Friday night. No one would be there for a couple of days. I laid down under the table and hoped I could just somehow go away.

Minutes later, I still wasn't dead.

FUCK! Fuck, fuck, fuck. I don't want to go back to that life. It was an empty feeling. No part of my life, even the possibility of dying, was making me feel better. I was ready to give up on this too. I didn't feel like I had accomplished anything in my life and couldn't even accomplish ending it that night.

Well, what the hell do I do now? I suppose I should go back to the pool house so they won't have to spend a bunch of time looking for me. I walked back into the pool house to the storage space behind the shower and crawled amongst all the water toys. There was a huge stack of blow-up floaties and lounge chairs. I dug my way into the middle of the pile to hide. I figured if I could just suck it up and stay here for a day or so, somehow, some way, I would eventually die. Enough blood had to eventually make its way out of me, right? *Maybe a lack of calories will finish the job.* I dozed off.

The next thing I knew, somebody was shaking me. "Blue. Blue. Wake up, buddy. Wake up. We gotta go. We gotta get you out of here." He was on the concrete floor, on the other side of the blood-stained shower stall, below a bunch of colorful children's floaties, right there with me.

Shit. Sonofabitch. I'm still alive, and now people know. Dammit.

Well, there was no sense in avoiding it. The jig was up. I stood up and went with my cousin, one arm around my waist, his other hand pulling my arm over his shoulders.

Wait a sec. What was this? Sandy's car was out of the garage and backed up in the driveway? *Huh?*

Jacques put me in the passenger seat. He looked at Sandy and said, "This is not good." Then he shut the door and got in behind me, his hands resting on my shoulders, comforting me, stabilizing me, securing me.

I looked at Sandy. She knew. I leaned my head on the window next to me. Staring off into nothing, I felt embarrassed, disappointed, lost, and still in a daze.

It was over. The pretending that I was fine, acting like things were great. The wishing that I could just get through this. The attempts at change. The hoping that the pot at the end of the rainbow would just surface and magically make everything OK.

It was all over. I was starting over.

My wife and cousin carried me into the hospital. As I walked through the door, the staff took me and got me onto a bed. All of a sudden, it felt like dozens of people were swirling around me. Bringing in equipment. Hooking things up to me and poking stuff into me. Asking questions. Writing on clipboards. Checking out various parts of my body.

I was hungover and short on blood. My brain was spinning. I wasn't really able to focus on any one thing since it seemed even more was stirring inside me than in the emergency room.

Someone in hospital worker garb kept asking me how I was doing. Seemed like I had to tell them my name every fifteen minutes. Another person kept talking, giving me a play-by-play of everything they were doing. "OK, we're going to get an IV set up for you. Gotta check your pulse. You're in the hospital. When's your birthday?"

I'm not a first-grader. I got it—you're worried about me. I'm fine. They clearly disagreed.

I couldn't feel anything. Anything physically, that is. Inside I was all discombobulated. *What just happened? What is happening now? What is all the fuss about?*

I knew I tried to kill myself, but I continued to think, *What's the big deal? Life sucked, and I tried to end it. Simple as that. Who doesn't get that?*

Except it seemed to everyone in the room that it was a big deal. A doctor or a nurse confirmed that I'd cut my wrists attempting suicide. No, it wasn't an accident, I told them. Yes, I'd been drinking. I described how it happened. For me, this was all so matter-of-fact.

At some point, I must have been stabilized because they asked if I wanted to see anyone.

"No."

A while later, they came back to say, "There are people who want to see you."

Well, I didn't want to see them.

"No."

This back and forth went on forever, it seemed, just painfully long, until I finally realized that it was time to face the music.

I was so incredibly embarrassed. *How could I have let this happen?* I tried to kill myself and failed. *Why did I even try if I wasn't going to go through with it?* This was worse than not even trying at all. Now I had to explain to everyone what was going on with me.

Except I still didn't know, didn't really fully understand. *What the hell was wrong with me?*

I couldn't see Sandy. I just couldn't. For months, the only thing that had been holding me back from committing suicide was that I knew how cruel it would be to leave her. My dad left me, and this would even be worse. I would be gone-gone. Like my mom, Todd, Scott. Not just halfway across the country. *What was I supposed to say to this woman that I loved?* I knew I hurt her. Bad. There was no way I could face her.

I asked for my brother. What he thought didn't matter. We were stuck with each other. Always have been, always will be.

There were tears in his eyes when he walked in. *He's a big dude, and he's crying? Wow, I must have hurt him. Did I?* I figured I did, but how could I have hurt him? *Seriously—how? It's not like I took a blade to his wrists.*

He looked me straight in the eye and said in no uncompromising terms, "This is a game-changer." We didn't say anything after that. He just put his hand on my shoulder and asked if I was ready to see Sandy. I supposed it was time. Couldn't avoid it any longer. I took a deep breath and told him, "Fine."

When she walked in, I turned my head, unable to look her in the eye. She was crying. I was still fairly emotionless. We talked about what to do next. Neither of us knew. The doctors said I needed to stay in the hospital. That made no sense to me. I don't need to stay in the hospital. She said I didn't have a choice.

What have I done? What have I done?

"What about the kids?" I asked. I must have suspected the answer because that's when I lost it.

I couldn't be away from the kids, I told her. I just couldn't. I needed to be with the kids. I couldn't go to bed under a different roof than them. I fought it. I argued with her, with the psych specialists, with the doctors. I would change. I know I have a problem. I tried to say anything so they would let me go home and be with the kids. I begged and pleaded, but it was useless. I was staying in the hospital.

The lady from the psych unit came back and confirmed it. She was gentle, but she let me know I didn't have a choice. They needed to watch me. I was not happy about that one bit. I knew I was depressed and needed to stop drinking. But this? Staying at the hospital seemed a little excessive to me.

The next thing I knew, I woke up in a different room in the hospital. I learned that I was in the psychiatry section of Overlake Hospital. The psych ward. *One Flew Over the Cuckoo's Nest.* It didn't feel like that to me. Nobody was strutting around like a chicken. Except that's what it was.

How was I psycho? How did I get this way? How did I let myself get this way? I still felt like me. I still couldn't figure out how I'd made the leap from there, the old me, to here, this me.

I stayed a few days under the watch of Overlake's psychiatric department. Ate. Talked. Took a survey or two. *What the hell were those for? They were going to say I was depressed and drank too much. No revelation there.* But I didn't ask why I was taking them or what they were for. I just did as I was told. I didn't know how long I was staying, but I didn't ask to leave. Didn't question much of anything at all.

There was a community room with tables and chairs, which I sat in, and activities, which I didn't participate in. There was more sleeping. More questions. More eating. More sleeping.

Surreal.

My wife visited me more than once during my first couple of days there. She started talking about what to do next and let me know she was researching alcohol recovery centers.

What?

Alcohol wasn't my problem, I told myself. Having Depression was. I didn't need to go to some AA place. I needed help with my sadness and feeling lost and angry and depressed.

Sure, it wouldn't hurt to stop drinking, but I could handle that on my own.

I was already full of solutions.

My wife said: "I don't trust you at home with the kids. I don't trust you by yourself. I need you under 24/7 supervision."

Ouch. Holy shit. Harsh.

But I couldn't argue with her anymore. It was a good call, and I understood. I had really fucked up. My mind was in this odd place. There was some feeling that I, the outwardly successful part, shouldn't be there. That wasn't how my life was supposed to go. But that aspect of my thinking was very small compared to the part that just didn't know much of anything. Didn't care about much of anything. No plan. No expectations. No curiosity. No ideas. I was merely existing at this point.

Someone came in to talk with me about alcoholism and recommended a place in Kirkland that I'd heard of. I played baseball against the American Legion baseball team it sponsored in high school. There were other options, one in Oregon and one in eastern Washington. Those two sounded better to me. Away from anyone I might know. But Milam was fifteen minutes from Sandy and the kids. They could visit me on the weekends.

"OK," I said. That would be our next step, inpatient recovery at a place for addicts.

The final question while at the hospital was whether or not I would go home for a night or go straight to alcoholism treatment. I really wanted to go home. *Just one night. Let me see the kids. Please let me see the kids.*

The doctor, the alcoholism expert, and my wife all said I should just go straight to inpatient recovery. That hurt. I bawled. I was losing my kids.

What had I done? What was going on? I argued as best I could. There was no way I was going to four weeks of recovery without seeing my kids. I just couldn't handle it. I had already been away from them for five nights.

Their argument was that I could skip town. Or drink. Or do something to disrupt, or even not start, my recovery. I was still convinced that alcohol wasn't the problem. I "knew" that I wouldn't drink or run away.

Then again, what the hell did I know at that point? I did understand Sandy's position. After all, I did just try to kill myself.

Eventually, they won out, and I went straight from Overlake Hospital in Bellevue to Milam Recovery Center in Kirkland. It was just a few miles away from my home, and across the street from Juanita High School.

How far I've come.

PART 2

UP

CHAPTER 7

Support

Upon entering the rehab center for the first time, all I saw was a grimy, poorly kept, cheap motel. Worn. Dust bunnies and spiderwebs in the corners. I was expecting decent hotel quality. Not as nice as some of the places I'd be accustomed to on business trips, but something clean and maintained. This was not that. With every passing minute, each step I took further into the place, the more and more pissed off I felt. *What the hell was I doing here?* Maybe I was an alcoholic, but I wasn't a drunk. I didn't do drugs. *This was such bullshit.*

A kind gentleman checked me in, got me set up in my room, and then checked on me a few times over my first couple of days. He joked around, had a very friendly demeanor. I thought he was a jackass. I had started a journal when I got there and included my thoughts about him. He was dumb, everyone around me was awful, and the place was just plain horrible.

They must have read the journal because I could tell something was wrong. The next time I saw him, he just bowed his head and walked by. That was my first wake-up call. I felt awful. He was being kind, and I was getting all high and mighty. *C'mon Blue, these people are just trying to help.*

The schedule at the recovery center was pretty strict. Up at 7 a.m., lights out at 11 p.m. kind of a deal. Thirty-minute windows for breakfast, lunch, and dinner. Felt like every quarter-hour was planned, even the free time. It wasn't jail, and it wasn't the military, but it sure wasn't the real world either.

In the evenings, we all got together in a big room for a lecture or presentation or video. People shared their stories of becoming lost and found. We watched documentaries about the chemistry and biology of the disease called alcoholism and the broader problem of addiction. Sometimes there were just talks from various experts and seasoned recovery veterans. They shared ideas about what to do when you got out, how to get back to living life, what to watch out for. A couple of nights each week, we were driven to Alcoholics Anonymous meetings, the type of which and with whom we went were chosen for us based on what they thought fit our situation.

On Sundays, families could visit. One night a week, spouses or significant others came for a joint meeting, as much to inform them as it was us.

I slept a full eight hours a night and, on many days, added a nap. I also chowed every meal they put in front of me. The food was not healthy, but the portions were just right. There were no snacks. I lost weight while I was there.

After a few days, I started working exercise into my afternoons. They had a path that circled the campus, which I walked or jogged. One afternoon I decided to extend my walk outside the property. Up the hill in one direction, then down to the end of the block in another direction. I had a feeling I shouldn't be doing it, but no one had ever told me outright that I couldn't. I wanted to press a little.

I got called into the principal's office the next day, so to speak. I knew why they called me in and was slightly frustrated. *I am a grown man. I know what I'm doing. This place is ridiculous.*

One of the recovery center leaders chastised me a bit about leaving campus. Did I know the rules? "Yes, but I didn't think it was a big deal." She reminded me of the reasoning behind the rules, which I understood. She questioned if I was committed to sticking it out.

Surprisingly, midmeeting, I realized I was committed. I didn't want to leave rehab just quite yet. I got concerned. My skin warmed up a little. *Are they going to kick me out?* I didn't want that. Feelings of remorse crept in and surprised me. Not that I left campus, necessarily, but that I broke the rules of this place that was trying to help me out. I pushed a little too far.

After leaving the office, I walked down the hallway, wondering what was happening to me. I felt less resentment, maybe even a bit of a bond with the place, and was prepared for more. Something was shifting. Maybe I actually needed that place.

I started to get a bit of a routine back to my life. That they planned our schedule and took care of meals was uncomfortable at first, sure, but it relieved some of the pressure of having to think about that kind of stuff on my own. They created an environment that was all about recovery, nothing else.

Eventually, instead of pushing back against every suggestion they made, I joined in. I had been assigned a counselor and spent time in both one-on-one and group meetings with him.

The group meetings were especially eye-opening for me. About six of us, plus the counselor, sat in a circle and talked. We would get assignments with questions and topics meant to open our Selves up to exploration and discussion one day, then present them the following meeting. Some were introductory in nature, where we grew up, when we started abusing drugs. Others were deeper, how we hurt ourselves, who we hurt around us.

I discovered that, in this sense, we really weren't all that different from each other. The methods, duration, and specifics might differ. Our ages and financial situations may vary. In the end, though, we were just trying to figure out ourselves, our place in the world, and how we were going to move forward.

I really dove into this part of the program, over time relishing it. I enjoyed sharing stories and asking questions about each person's struggles with whatever dependence they had or whatever personal issues they were trying to work through. I listened and tried to apply their stories to mine. I worked to find a little nugget that might shed light on what was going on with me. Searching for clues that might lead me to feel in any way possible better than what I felt before rehab.

The only thing that might have made me different than my group mates was my desire. I knew I wanted to get better, and I knew I wanted to stop drinking, no question. I didn't sense a similar level of aspiration from everyone in the group or even across the entire rehab facility. Some seemed like they were done with their old selves, but I'm not sure that most felt that way.

We talked about RET, rational emotive therapy. A method for changing one's perception of circumstances. Instead of focusing on how a situation might be bad, could there be another way to look at it? Instead of viewing situations as always or never, we learned to recognize them as sometimes or maybe. I learned about CBT, cognitive behavioral therapy. It is a similar recovery tool that works to change our perceptions and reactions to the world around us and our lives within it.

These tools, strategies, were so interesting to me. Not that I completely bought off on the idea that just one of them was going to magically make me feel better. But that they existed. That something else was out there that could be the answer, or part of the answer. It wasn't just me anymore, trying to figure this out from scratch.

Before rehab, I would poo-poo this sort of psychobabble. Eventually, though, I let my curiosity take over. Maybe I was finally ready to begin my recovery. I began to reflect, asking internal questions. What could possibly be in it for me? What might apply to me? What feels like it might work for me long-term?

When I started looking at the discussions, videos, and readings as opportunities instead of hassles, I felt better about rehab. I stopped focusing on the fact that the food wasn't all organic and whole and started realizing that having three square meals a day prepared for me was pretty nice. I stopped getting frustrated that I was a grown man being told to go to bed and started being grateful that I was getting proper sleep. I stopped being upset that they didn't spend more time on physical health and began to appreciate the leisurely strolls I could take each afternoon. I stopped resenting the fact that I spent my evenings in meetings where I was learning something, rather than out at a bar.

The biggest thing I was *not* upset over? The absence of alcohol. Boy, it was so nice. What a relief. I didn't have to pretend to be "Shots of Jack Guy" anymore. I didn't have to think about what I would drink, where I would drink, or how I would act after getting drunk. No more internal struggles about drinking or not drinking, feeling good or bad about either decision. By that point, every decision I was making about alcohol was the wrong one. Here, there were no more wrong decisions, no more decisions on that front at all.

About three weeks in, I went back to my room, and the owner was waiting for me. He was the founder's son, an old buddy from the Greek system. I remember thinking, in college, *that guy might be able to drink as much as me, maybe more.* He had stopped drinking alcohol years ago and took over the family business of helping people with their addictions. He said he had seen my name on a roster and wanted to give his personal support. I couldn't believe it. I thought that was so generous of him. He ran several recovery centers in the Seattle area, and for him to take time to wish me well and offer assistance, well, that meant a lot.

After four weeks at the substance abuse recovery center and one week in the psych ward at the hospital, I was through with the first step of my recovery. I had accepted the fact that I had both alcoholism and depression. I had discussed my suicide attempt enough times that it became real. I had cleared my system of a lot of alcohol.

With very little fanfare, I headed home and said goodbye to the first of many support networks I've had in my life since my attempt.

Removing alcohol from my system helped me feel much better physically, but didn't cure the symptoms that often accompanied depression and Depression. I spent most of my thirties getting sick three or four times a year for seven to ten days at a time. Head colds. Congestion. Flu. Fever. Everyday American sicknesses that we all seem to accept as part of life. Mine just felt intensified, a little more severe. It was just so frustrating.

During the deepest valleys of my Depression, I calculated I lost weeks of living every year because of these sicknesses. I would visit the doctor and either get a recommendation to drink fluids and get some rest (*duh*), or get a prescription for antibiotics. *That's it?* While being hungover and feeling down, I took advantage of the colds and sickness. I didn't really want to tackle the day anyway, so I used a head cold as an excuse to extend my blah feelings a few days.

During rehab, one of the conclusions I came to was that I wanted to become well, totally well. All of me. I was turned off by the lack of interest in my overall health from the myriad of general practitioners I talked with. No doctor I visited seemed curious enough to ask why I got sick. They seemed uninterested in stopping the sickness before it started or perhaps recommending a lifestyle change. They just wanted to treat the illness. I wanted a doctor who focused on my health, not my sickness. I did not want to walk into another doctor's office and hear a form of the question, "What type of drug would you like?"

I am here—again—for the same thing. Let's figure this out. That was my line of thinking.

In my twenties, I learned about naturopathy and homeopathy from my Aunt Kay. In Seattle, alternatives to traditional Western medicine were more available and acceptable than in other parts of the country, though, in the '90s, they were still a little out there.

A high school and college buddy of mine who I deeply respected had gone to Bastyr, the top naturopathic medicine school in the country, to become a naturopathic doctor. I would have loved to see him. The only problem was that his practice was about an hour away. So, as one of the first steps I took after getting out of rehab, I looked for NDs closer to me.

I found Dr. Rinde through internet searches. He went to Bastyr, a check in the plus column, but what pushed him over the top for me was that he had worked for the University of Arizona Athletic Department. A naturopath with an athletic background? Sign me up.

Our first meeting lasted over an hour, where I shared much of my life story, including my suicide attempt. He asked a variety of typical questions about my physical health. Then he took it a step further. He probed into the timing of when my emotional state began its turn for the worst. He took an interest in the whole of me from childhood through adulthood and into my current living situation. He wanted to know about my nonphysical well-being. For the first time, I connected with a doctor who seemed interested in my wellness, not my sickness. With each of his questions, I became more hopeful. *Maybe this guy is going to actually try to help me.*

The first thing he wanted to address was my physical situation. He felt that physical limitations were impeding the progress of my emotional and spiritual recovery. He talked with me about the idea that stressors brought about by extreme negative emotions had caused inflammation. Toxins were floating around in my body that needed to be flushed out. The physical manifestation of my emotional distress was tangible.

The first thing he had me do was go through a twenty-one-day detox and elimination diet. Though I was extremely excited and motivated, it was not easy. The first few days were excruciating as I took caffeine out of my system. The worst headaches I'd ever experienced. Complete drug withdrawal that lasted about ten days.

Some of the diet was straightforward. Mix a powder with liquid and drink up. Grocery shopping and meal planning were more complicated. Every few days, the list of what I could and couldn't eat changed. After so many foods had been eliminated, the monotony set in. I kept telling myself that this would take fewer days than rehab.

When I was done, though, I felt like I'd completed a year's worth of recovery in just three weeks. Both my physical and my nonphysical Self had improved. It was as much of a transformation as had occurred during my twenty-eight days in rehab, just a monumental shift in my wellness.

Over the last ten years, I've continued working with the same naturopath to fend off any recurrence of Depression that might sprout, improve and optimize my overall wellness, and relieve the minor physical ailments that occur over time. We do bloodwork at least every twelve months, trying to dial in what I'm eating and doing. He continues to check in on my entire life, well-being, and goals. When he proposes a solution, it is something sustainable, not a stopgap measure just to get me through the next few days.

He has helped me think about preventative medicine. He helped me think about the entire body as being connected, that it must work together, with no single part of me functioning on its own. He factors in my nonphysical state as much as my physical. We work on me being the best me possible through all of life's changes.

I feel like he's my secret weapon.

Not drinking took so much of my focus and energy, but I knew that sobriety was just the beginning of my nonphysical health. Instinctively, I still believed my Depression was an even more significant issue than the alcoholism. It had to be addressed if I were to be well and stay out of the darkness.

A few months after my attempt, the couple's counselor that my wife and I had been seeing recommended a men's group. She thought I might fit in with the eight to ten middle-aged men who formed the group. All of them were working through the aftermath that shadows addiction or dependency. They met once a week for ninety minutes, and most of the men had years of recovery. That's all I knew about this specific group going in. But I had learned, at rehab, that I enjoyed and grew from talking in a group. That gave me hope, so I decided to join.

On a Thursday night, I parked in front of the '70s-style building and wondered how close to an AA meeting this was going to be. Some parts of AA worked for me, but most of it didn't, so I wanted this group to be different. I followed the hallway to a small therapist's office overlooking manmade Lake Bellevue. It was a peaceful setting full of dark wood and leather and about eight men sitting in a circle. Though I felt like the youngest one there, I wasn't out of place.

The meeting started, as they all did, with everyone providing a standard check-in. Just a few minutes each, letting the others know how they were doing that week. For the first meeting, I was told I could skip that part to gain an understanding of what the introductory period was all about. I would then introduce myself.

When it came time for me to speak up, I just let it all hang out, just like I did after a few weeks at the rehab center. I told the others about my suicide attempt, drinking, Depression, and loss. I rambled on about why I was there and how I got there. Bam. Just threw it out there.

After I was done talking, I paused and looked up. I sensed it was a lot for them. They all were very polite, welcomed me into the group, and thanked me for sharing. I later learned that not everyone was as comfortable as I, putting their story out on the line right from the get-go. Some men showed up and wouldn't talk for weeks. Others just shared little bits and pieces of their lives or spoke superficially, seemingly never becoming comfortable getting into the depths of how they were feeling.

My introduction felt good, though, and I was glad I did it. I was there to figure it all out. And if I didn't start talking about the "it," how could it be figured out? If that was wrong, I wouldn't last long anyway.

That weekly Thursday night meeting became a cornerstone for my recovery. We all talked about our addiction or drug dependency and whether we were putting ourselves in a position for a setback. But the drugs were never the focus. It didn't feel that way for me, at least.

Everyone in the group had a career to manage and a family to support. Each guy had life concerns that he brought to the meetings. Not every guy every time, but each shared something they were working on that was bigger than not drinking or drugging over time. The ideas, questions, and stories shared were done so in the hope of finding a path toward wellness.

In the beginning, I felt like such a taker. I was trying to figure out life without alcohol, my next career, and my Depression. I always had something to share. Every one of those men offered valuable support to me throughout my time with them. It could have been a brief, "Yep, I've been there," to a book suggestion, a something-to-think-about, or an action to take. Issues with my parenting? At least one of them could commiserate and discuss what worked or didn't work with them. Death in the family? Struggling to be comfortable at a party? Challenging relationship? Of the four to eight other men in the group, one would always have a piece of wisdom to share. Even the simple acknowledgment that they genuinely understood what I was talking about was tremendous.

It was comforting having a regular discussion with guys who knew me, who I completely trusted, but who weren't in my regular social circle. It allowed for a more open, frank discussion. Not a lot of small talk or bullshit. We were all taking time out of our busy lives, so we did not mess around. We got straight to issues and areas that were really important.

Eventually, I felt like I was contributing as much as I was receiving. Most nights, almost every night, I left the meeting feeling inspired. I liked knowing men who were interested in improving their lives. Knowing that others had daily struggles helped me get through my own. Feeling as if I might have contributed to someone else's positive steps forward was uplifting. It motivated me to take care of my life.

I ended up leaving the group after our twins were born. The meeting was during their dinner-bath-homework-reading routine, time that was too valuable to me. Plus, I wanted to share it with my wife. I had learned by watching my older two just how quickly each childhood phase passes.

I had to let my men's group go.

When I told the group what I needed to do, I shared that the most important thing for my personal wellness was supporting my family. I felt that I had made tremendous strides in the past four years and that I would be OK going out on my own.

There was some consternation from others. There was the reminder that you can't stop doing what got you to a good place. This is true, but life does evolve as well, they acknowledged. In the end, they supported me in leaving.

I remained in contact with a few of the men and the moderator, who made it clear he was always available to us, anytime. I've talked with some over the phone, but there was one who I connected with the most, and it surpassed recovery. I still see him in person for walk-'n'-talks regularly. We bond over art, sports, parenting, current events, whatever comes up in our lives. He is the light being carried forward from that group of inspiring men.

Besides this group therapy, I also had a weekly, one-on-one, sixty-minute session with a therapist. I knew that continuing therapy work was imperative for my well-being. I didn't know how it would work, but my positive experience at the recovery center replaced the negative experience with my initial therapists, so I had hope. One of the first things I did after rehab was search for the right personal therapist. I finally settled on Dale.

Dale's office was close to my house, so there would be less impediment to going. His office was warm but not too stereotypically "therapy." He didn't look like a therapist. He just looked like a nice guy, a friendly face with warm eyes.

During the first few sessions, I wasn't solely focused on getting better. I was just trying to find the right person for this critical piece of my recovery. As much as I would answer his questions, I would analyze the questions themselves. *Was he asking good questions? Why was he asking them? Who is doing more talking here?* I would assess the meeting not in its outcome but in the method. *Was this the way out?*

Almost subversively, Dale's approach was working. I just kept showing up, and I just kept feeling better. I met with Dale and I didn't want my life to end. The outcome was so simple because the input was almost just as simple. It worked because he focused on getting me through the day and the week. That was it. I had never thought like that before.

He didn't focus on my dad or my mom, or alcohol, or grieving, or anything in the past. He didn't focus on goals or ambitions or the future either. It was all about today. Right now. What was in front of me, and what was on the forefront of my mind. That approach felt so right, a Goldilocks approach just for me, and was unique in my limited experience. It was almost as if he was saying: "Let's not try to figure this all out at once. Let's just make it through the day until the next time we get together." I really needed to hear that. Frankly, it was all I could handle during the first couple of years of my recovery.

For years that weekly therapy session became so critical to my wellness. More than trying to uncover issues from the past, it was a time when I could reflect on my own progress against whatever expectation I was setting for myself at the time. Most of the time, that reflection was limited to the past week, sometimes only the past day or two. How did I feel I was doing? How did I feel about how I felt? Was I giving myself a chance at getting healthy?

Those are questions I could have asked of myself alone. Having a professional to keep me in check made the reflection session so much more productive. I couldn't get off on random tangents. If I was misconstruing a situation, someone was there to check me on it. We even spent time reflecting on my plan for the next few days.

From time to time, Dale would give me some homework, articles to read, or topics to explore. Through his gentle, caring prodding, I learned about mindfulness, accepting emotions, and self-esteem.

For most of my adult life, I thought I knew everything. If I didn't know something, it either didn't matter or I would figure it out on my own. This was such a huge step in building my wellness foundation. Allowing someone else to teach me about me, acknowledging that I still had so much to learn, accepting that there may be different perspectives out there.

Sometime during that first year of recovery, which was probably closer to a year than six months, I was ready to open up to my friends again. It felt like years since I'd done that. In Depression, I stopped feeling like talking. I didn't answer the phone. I was either angry at the world, which meant anything they might say would be deemed idiotic, or I was so down I couldn't even summon the energy to make small talk.

I used the lessons I learned in rehab and forced myself to open up to the idea that I could once again connect with my old friends. Listen, share, talk. I was going to do it, but I sure was nervous at first.

I was so lucky to have so many friends, but a few occasions stick out for me.

There was the message from Steve, the other Kirkland roommate with Scott. A few months after getting home from rehab, I picked up a voicemail from him. "We heard about what happened and just want you to know that we are here for you if you need anything at all." That was it. So simple, but so timely and meaningful.

There was the sit-down I had with Steve Hardie a couple of months after my attempt. It was the first time I'd seen him since that night. We beat around the bush for a little while, with some catching-up small talk, until a moment of silence. He just looked at me and said, "I'm pissed at you." I stared at him, trying to read him. I knew he was being honest. "You don't get to do that. You don't get to take the easy way out and leave me."

Wow. *Thank you so much for saying that straight to my face.* I knew exactly what he meant and where he was coming from. And I knew he understood my pain and my decision. I was reminded that this friend was family. I knew he would be with me no matter what. I was also given a ray of hope. Maybe I, too, could have the courage to talk straight with someone someday. *I sure hope I don't have to have this talk with him.*

About eleven months after my attempt, my first birthday following, my wife took me out to dinner in Seattle's South Lake Union area. As we walked into the restaurant, my oldest friend and one of the best people I know walked down the stairs with his girlfriend. "What are you doing here!? What a coincidence!" I said. They said they were going to the same restaurant as me. How could this be? How cool is this? We walked into the restaurant, and my brother and his wife were sitting at a table. Another one of my best friends, the one I call my adopted brother, was there with his wife. I finally figured it out. They were here for me.

Almost a year into recovery, I was still pretty out of it.

How thoughtful of Sandy to arrange this dinner. How brave. Who knows how I might have reacted? I still wasn't ready for this, to be out with a group of people, but I just took it in. If any group was going to help me along with my first steps back into the world, these people were going to be part of it.

Then there was The Weekly Call.

Craig became one of my best friends between late elementary school and junior high. We lived a few blocks from each other and did everything together. Played multiple sports. Rode our bikes to school and practice and the nearest minimart, where there happened to be *Asteroids* and *Space Invaders* in the garage. We played hours of wiffle ball with our brothers. We had sleepovers that included rock 'n' roll, Risk, and Heather Thomas and Farrah Fawcett posters.

He moved away, I moved away, and we lost contact for several years. Then, not long after I got out of rehab, seemingly out of nowhere, he just started calling me. And kept calling me. He'd leave a short message, and then he'd call again, a week or so later. I still wasn't feeling entirely social or connected to people yet. I wasn't feeling too confident in myself at that time. But I really liked Craig, he was part of my chosen family, and it was fun to catch up with an old friend.

Months down the road, the conversations got longer. We were both stay-at-home dads and could talk during the day when most of our friends were at their office jobs. We started scheduling our calls for a specific time on a specific day. I became more and more comfortable talking with him and began to actually look forward to our calls.

Eventually, it dawned on me that Craig was calling as a way of supporting me. We never talked about Depression, or drinking, or grieving, or much of anything outside of sports and kids. Maybe the occasional current event or political topic. But the call was always there. Craig was always there.

After sitting with this realization for a while, I summoned the courage to say something. To acknowledge what he had been doing for me.

As one phone call was closing down, I said, "Craig, you've been calling me regularly for a long time now." I stumbled a bit because I wasn't sure how to say what I hoped he would hear. "I just want you to know how much I appreciate it. I didn't realize it at first, but now I know how much you've been supporting me. How you've been keeping up on me."

Long pause.

Then he just said, "I have my friend back."

Another pause.

I didn't know what to say. I had no idea that I'd been that far gone. I thought we just fell apart over time like old friends tend to do. I was blown away. How great of a thing was that to hear?

I just said, "Thank you," and hung up. Then I wept.

I thought, *where had I been*? Had it been that obvious? What had I become? Fortunately, I'd grown enough that I didn't dwell on the sort of thinking that could turn into regret. I just accepted his comment for what it was.

Those little gestures held such great power. A quick message, releasing the elephant from the room. Brutal honestly coming straight from the heart. Just showing up.

I was not alone. Beyond my own cognition, people were looking out for me.

During that initial recovery phase, I even had to become comfortable leaning on my wife, which should have been easier. She seemed to have more faith in me than I did in myself.

During so much of the time I struggled with my internal turmoil, I felt like the spiritual connection I had with my wife was fading. Through the fog of Depression, I could no longer see or feel this woman I was infatuated with. This woman who I couldn't get enough of, whose presence I just wanted to be around. Even Sandy, my love, was a shadow.

With regular therapy and alcohol removed, she came back into vision. Once I was able to see her again, I started to realize that she played the most critical role of all in my recovery. She enabled me to find my own way home.

I think about it like this:

I picture a moment in our wedding when we were being hitched together, literally, with a rope looped between us. When we said "I do," I envisioned that rope tied between us.

With both of us fairly ambitious, I likened aspects of our relationship to a mountain climb. Neither of us was an extreme risk-taker, nor did we lean to the spontaneous side. We didn't choose the path that went straight up the rock face. Life, for us, wasn't a bunch of switchbacks either. We were taking a more systematic path to the top. We picked a trail that gradually spiraled upward around the mountain. Always going up, taking in all of the views as we went, and never stressing us out too much. At least that seemed to be the initial plan, the one we agreed to when we got engaged, so we walked together for the first few thousand feet.

At some point, I ventured from the original plan. I began to wonder what it might be like if I just went straight up the side. I left Steady Sandy and scrambled up on my own.

"It's beautiful up here!" I yelled down to Sandy. "You can see forever!"

"Great," she would say smiling, as she stayed true to the plan and just kept walking upward.

Then I would come barreling down the mountain to find her and be with her. But my momentum would carry me past the trail down to where we had just been. Breathing hard and scratched from the brush and trees off the path, I would stagger back to join Sandy and continue the even climb. Pretty soon, I would again become antsy, and up the mountain I would go, again finding joy in the elevation. But now, a bit wearier with a compass not as true, my trek back down would take longer, I would miss my wife and would fall deeper down the other side of the trail.

I continued this pattern. Up the hill on top of the world, then falling farther back down into the unknown. Sandy and I grew farther apart, but she just kept giving me slack. Until finally, one day, I stumbled so far down and hurt myself so badly that I was having trouble getting back up. I was face down in some swampy, bug-infested, dark, thick muck. Not moving.

I felt Sandy tug at the rope, pulling and pulling with all her might. Eventually, she stopped pulling, maybe realizing that she wasn't going to be able to pull me up if I wasn't going to do some climbing myself.

She never untied the rope between us, though. Sandy didn't go back down the mountain. She didn't try to force me to do anything. She did make sure I could see her. She let me know she was still there by tugging on the rope periodically. She waited. But she never untied the rope. She never let go of me. Sandy never let me just leave my face in the muck for good.

CHAPTER 8

Alcoholism

I wanted to stop drinking for years. I tried to take my own life after drinking a year's worth of tequila shots in one night. It didn't require much convincing for me to realize that I needed to stop drinking alcohol for good this time.

It wasn't straightforward, and I may have ventured from a proven path, but I didn't have a huge struggle with being sober. It wasn't a slam dunk, it took some getting used to, but I was never really concerned I would relapse.

I took on a binary view of things. I was a better person when I didn't drink, and I was a worse person when I did drink. That was level one. If I ever questioned level one, I went to a deeper, more powerful line of thinking. Drinking equals death. It became that simple. The details were irrelevant. Just don't drink, then I can live and get better.

I floundered through the actions. Talked to myself in different ways. Read a variety of books and articles. Tried on different perspectives. But the core reasoning never wavered. I was done drinking.

It took about a year for me to feel physically different. It was as if there were layers of alcohol that needed to be removed. Toxins in my skin, in my organs, in my joints. Those were the first to get peed or sweated out. Then came the toxins that were in my brain, my heart, and my spirit. That took more time and effort, but they eventually worked their way out as well.

Learning about the science and biology of alcohol and alcoholism helped me make sense of living with the disease. What the drug does to your brain. How your body deals with alcohol. What alcohol is made of and the toxins in alcoholic beverages. What makes alcohol addictive and how that translates to alcoholism in some.

All of that education helped to fortify my lizard-level thinking. It helped me understand just how awful a cheap well drink is for my health. Those dive bars and honky-tonks that I so loved, with their two- and three-dollar wells? Couldn't get enough of them. I would grab my drink and think *this twenty-dollar bill is gonna last me all day!* With my newfound knowledge, that whiskey and Coke looked a whole lot worse than just an alcoholic beverage.

I wish there were some kind of test for alcoholism, like an allergy test. The doctor pricks your back for peanuts, gluten, and alcohol. Or something like a pregnancy test. Pee on a stick and a red or green dot shows up. But there isn't a test. Just anecdotal evidence. Correlations. Intuition. Good ol' gut instinct. For some, alcoholism is binary. You either have it, or you don't. Based on my experience, the hours of discussion and reading, the years of living with me drinking and not drinking, my perception is that there are different varieties of alcoholism. It is a spectrum. My type of alcoholism isn't unique. Millions have it. But it is not the same as every person who has some form of alcoholism.

It sure would be nice if there was a test to give us more indication about what we're dealing with. Since there isn't, living with alcoholism takes education, time, reflection. I had to ask myself if one drink was worth it. I had to figure out why I wasn't going to drink. I had to reflect on what I was like when I was drunk and what I was like on the days I wasn't drinking. I had to think about the joy I found in life at age twenty-eight versus what I felt at age thirty-eight.

Those are all questions I had to ask myself. Sure, I paid attention to what other people were asking me. I listened when others were asked those types of questions. But in the end, it was up to me to determine where I stood on the drinking spectrum.

The saying, "If you have problems when you drink, you have a drinking problem," is at one end. Those problems can be mildish symptoms such as gaining unhealthy weight, losing your temper, or slacking off at work. Recognizing the problem and cutting back can be the solution for those at this end of the spectrum.

The chemical imbalance that causes addiction is at the extreme end. It is an addiction that demands to be fed, all day, every day. It causes paranoia and provokes deceit. This type of alcoholism must be dealt with more severely by being monitored while going through withdrawal, then continuing through a professionally run, intensive, inpatient rehab. No drinking is ever allowed. Major life changes, well beyond just sobering up, need to be confronted.

I fell somewhere in between. I had more than a drinking problem, but I wasn't addicted. I needed to make life changes, but I didn't need to go to AA every day. It is not an easy place to be in the alcoholism world. Things are pretty cut and dry here in general. But I've found my place, and I continue to find others who fall into the same alcoholism category as me.

Just removing alcohol from the equation made for an interesting first year of recovery. It was a regular activity simply to not think about alcohol, though I was fortunate that I hadn't become addicted to alcohol physically. I didn't have to fight through the sweats or the shakes. I wasn't thinking about not taking a sip every hour of every day. I can't imagine what that type of alcoholism must be like.

But I sure was addicted to alcohol and partying psychologically.

Because so much of my life revolved around alcohol, my effort and energy went beyond just abstaining. I needed to remind myself on Tuesday that I wasn't going out drinking on Thursday, or Friday, or Saturday. Any of those days. Ever. It required more energy than merely not drinking at an event. When I was telling other people no thanks, I was reminding myself, *No Way!*

Drinking alcohol is such an integrated part of society. Even though I felt confident in my decision, it didn't mean I wasn't prone to the regular internal dialogue. Just to realize that I wasn't going to drink again was this little burden that rode along with me like a pirate's parrot. *You can't drink. You aren't going to drink today. You aren't going to drink this weekend. Other people can have a drink or two, but you can't. Other people can pick out a bottle of wine with dinner, but you can't.* Those thoughts were always there, eating up cycles within my brain and soul.

Even though not drinking was an easy decision, living the life of a nondrinker was going to take some work. *Who doesn't drink?*

During that first year, I mainly avoided drinking situations. Every day, every week, every weekend, it got a little bit easier until eventually, I felt somewhat comfortable going to gatherings where people were drinking.

The second year of my sobriety was full of my nondrinking "firsts." First birthday party. First Cinco de Mayo. First Thanksgiving. I had to plow through all of those celebratory events— where even nondrinkers have a few—sober and smiling. I would look at the wet bar or the opened bottles of wine and think, *Nope, can't do that.*

I felt very fortunate that everyone around me was supportive. I never once had a buddy come up to me and say, "Just one. Come on. For old times' sake." I am so grateful I didn't have to go through that.

In fact, there were times I felt guilty because I knew how many eggshells had been spread on the floor before I entered. Guys who would typically be doing shots avoided that practice in front of me. At some point, it got funny because I would look around and notice my drinking buddies would be gone. Just minutes after standing in the kitchen telling stories with me, four guys would be out. Then they would come back in the house, through the kitchen door in plain sight, with shit-eating grins. I knew full well they had gone out back to do shots. I'd give them a look and say, "You think I don't know what you're doing?" They would look at me as if Dad just caught them, and we would laugh. I knew they were just trying to figure out this new guy who didn't have a bottle in his hand. They were acting as the good friends they were, and I needed that more than anything.

Another thing that kept me going day to day was some sense of pride. *Look at how well I'm progressing. Look at how healthy*

I'm being. I'm not going to act like a fool or hop behind the wheel. That felt good.

But mostly, it was just an internal back-and-forth dialogue. *How did I get here? Why can't I have one drink? It's not fair. Is the alcoholism in my blood or in my head? Just one drink. Why can't I have just one drink? I know I can't, but why?* I knew I had alcoholism, but I needed to work through those types of questions as part of the grieving process.

Though there is no one, specific alcoholism gene, it is understood in the medical community that alcoholism is hereditary. My dad likely had alcoholism. He sure was a sonofabitch when he drank. He tried to stop numerous times, eventually giving it up when he realized it would contribute to him landing in jail. My dad figured his dad had it. That guy, who I never met, was drunk all the time and beat his family, according to my dad. He died at an early age of liver complications. From my very first days of drinking, and probably before that, I figured I had alcoholism.

Another indicator that I have alcoholism is that I consume and respond to alcohol differently than most. My tolerance is like very few others I know. I don't have an off switch. After one drink, I crave two. After two, I crave four. After four, I crave all the drinks that might be available to me.

Alcohol acts as an upper to me, not the depressant it is. Maybe that's scientifically impossible, but that's sure how it feels. I realize that some people use alcohol at the end of the night to help calm themselves down, relax. I never understood that. All I wanted to do after a drink or two was have another drink or two.

But I didn't have the kind of alcoholism that craved booze throughout the day. I didn't feel a need for it to get me through the morning. I never had a bottle stashed. Never spent time sneaking drinks.

The personal education I went through in understanding the type of alcoholism I have was helpful in my recovery.

I envisioned all the bad that happened in my life as crude oil dumped layer upon layer into my heart. Eventually, the pressure of all of it hardened until my heart had a big lump of coal resting at the bottom. Not properly grieving, or even understanding what grieving was, let alone working through it, turned into a kind of reverse fracking. Not dealing with loss or change in a healthy way just pushed a bunch of dark, slimy, crud right down into the depths of my anatomy.

During my Depression, I pictured the alcohol washing off the top layer of gunk then carrying it through my blood vessels and into my brain, where it clouded everything. All I could see was that coal mine, dark and dusty, with death hanging at the top of the shaft. I could sit with that hard darkness for days, buried below all of the new light in my life, knowing full well that the next drink was going to wash it back into my system. My vision would become completely dark again.

The most significant indicator that I have alcoholism is that alcohol makes me look at the world differently. View everything through a dark lens. When it wasn't too bad, alcohol would trick me into thinking that my life was terrible. When it was really bad, alcohol would trick me into thinking that being alive is terrible.

I like the phrase, "I have alcoholism," because it sounds like the disease it is. "I'm an alcoholic," on the other hand, has such a negative connotation. The drunk. The guy with liquor on his breath who wakes up with a drink and continues to drink all day from stashed bottles. Who sweats when too little alcohol is in his system.

Such a distinction is important to me. Alcoholism vs. alcoholic. It is a mental shift that helps me manage not drinking in a society so curious about the nondrinker. The phrasing may sound unusual because it is not the norm, but it is accurate. "Having alcoholism" is akin to having celiac or having diabetes. It is something I have, not who or what I am.

It also helps when talking with others about my situation. Whether they are struggling with alcohol or just curious about those who do, if I use the phrase "They have alcoholism," I feel less strain or tension in the discussion. Some empathy exists, some entry-level of understanding.

"He's such an alcoholic," just feels disparaging.

So I tell people I have alcoholism. The person I say that most to is me.

There wasn't a single moment of clarity. Or a magical month, like, say, the twenty-fourth month, after which all of a sudden, I went, *I'm good, no thank you*. There was no "aha" moment when it no longer seemed a struggle. The contentment with not drinking just arrived, and my comfort level being in drinking environments just grew. Eventually, I brought back the parts of the drinking life I enjoyed without the negative impact of alcoholism. Whether at someone's home, or a music show, or a sporting event, I can easily slide into a party situation and hang out, carefree. I can hit a honky-tonk or club for live music and not feel one bit odd about the lack of a drink in my hand.

There are many days when I'm driving around, running errands, or chauffeuring my kids that I realize I wouldn't be doing this if I still drank. The old me could have easily stopped in and grabbed a quick one, and another for the road, while the kid was at a forty-five-minute gymnastics practice. I could easily slip a bit of whiskey in my coffee or Coke and sip on it for a few hours as I'm getting groceries and dropping off boxes at Goodwill.

Then I realize—no way. There's no way I would have this life if I kept drinking. Those things don't go together. There is no combination of alcohol-in-the-coffee-cup and laughing with my children in the car ride home. There is no swig off the bottle and trip to help someone else.

When it came to the end of my drinking career, it was about me and the alcohol. It consumed such a large part of my being.

Now it is about people and living. I have four kids who I support physically through actions such as cooking and driving, and emotionally through listening and discussing. I am not wasting their college funds on alcohol. I am not too foggy to really hear them. I am not too irritated and hung-over to support my wife. I'm physically healthier, probably above average for a guy my age. I have time for my family and friends. Quality time. I have patience, and I feel efficient.

The biggest thing that helps me feel good about not drinking is the understanding that I am choosing not to drink. I choose. There is power in that for me, even though there are times when I forget about that strength.

When I first walk into a bar. When my buddies order that first round. When the wine list is being passed around at the dinner table. Even after years of sobriety, my first reaction can be negative, a combination of regret and sorrow. Woe is me. Maybe the idea of drinking is still a habit. Maybe it is just instinctual, part of the disease.

However, with each passing year, thoughts like that enter my brain less often, stick around less long. I more quickly remember that I am making a choice. I choose to not drink. For my family. For my health. For my life. Those thoughts lift my spirits.

Even though so many amazing, beautiful things were happening to me as a result of not drinking, I knew that I still had deep, underlying issues—Depression, anger, regret, grieving—even after I cleansed my system of alcohol. It was a feeling, not really anything that could be tested. I just knew that I was unhealthy. Really unhealthy. As the months went by, my organs became more efficient, my brain started making new connections, and my heart was cleansed of that coal. These are all things that I wish we could measure scientifically. In reality, it is a spiritual feeling that sits in one's gut.

As the stream of alcohol was removed from my system, I began to feel differently. I had fewer aches and pains, and it was easier to fall asleep and get out of bed. My brain was able to begin the process of reworking itself. People weren't as dumb. There was less wrong in the world. That's when I started feeling different. About life. About my Self. Life became less about running from what I did and more about where I wanted to go, who I wanted to be. That would take more work, including facing other issues from my past.

CHAPTER 9

Grieving

When my dad took off for good that one night, there wasn't much time spent trying to understand how I felt about it. I was thirteen, my brother was ten, and my mom wasn't remotely prepared to become the breadwinner. She was overwhelmed. We were just trying to survive. There was no disposable income, nor time, for any kind of therapy, paid or otherwise. Given my mother's emotional state at the time, I can't imagine she was in any position to guide us through that trauma.

When Todd died, I was seventeen. No adult was living with me. Had I even processed any of the loss in my life that occurred up until then? Did I even know that I should try?

Then my mom died.

About a week after my mom died, I had a going-away party at the apartment in Juanita. Not a memorial. A party. At least that's how I looked at it. Laughing. Slamming drinks.

I left Kirkland and moved back in with my dad. I am certain that he knew nothing about dealing with grief or trauma in a supportive manner. He was incapable of sustained empathy or long-term, deep concern for others. For the next few months, I was having people over to my dad's house for beers. I drove around looking for fun with a twelve-pack in the trunk.

Six months after my mom died, I started digging graves for other dead people, hanging back, out of sight, as the grieving families paid their respects.

Then I went off to the fraternity for four years of drinking.

At this point in my life, staring at college, I was like a bloodied boxer who had just hit the floor but could stand back up. There was no way I was going to let the referee count all the way to ten, but I sure was having trouble finding my corner.

I certainly didn't consciously consider grieving for my mom, even if it was happening in the recesses of my mind. I also didn't think I was avoiding it. I just didn't talk with anyone about it, and no one brought it up with me.

Still, my life was pretty simple at this time. It was just me trying to put one foot forward. I could do that, regardless of the burdens I carried. I was strong enough for me. So I didn't try to unload them. I just learned to climb with them.

By the time I had a wife, a home, a couple of kids, and a career, those burdens had morphed themselves to me. They were just a part of me. Except now they felt heavier. I wanted to carry that other stuff. My family was the fun lifting. That old baggage was now taxing. On me and my life.

I wasn't prepared with even a rudimentary knowledge of what a grieving process was. For me, after everyone left, it was all about keeping going. Work, make money, tend to the kids, meet friends for drinks, set goals, achieve them, set higher goals. I was in perpetual motion, never stopping to grieve. Just go. Move forward.

I knew I felt sad. I accepted that I would feel sad. I expected it. I became very good at it. I could cry. Hard. Bawl like a baby. But that was it. I'd get all the sadness out and move on. Or that's what I told myself. I hoped and hoped that one day the sadness would just be gone. But the sadness never went away. That is what made me angry. I didn't get mad at the death, or the reason for the death. I got mad at the grief, or my lack of grieving, or whatever it was that was bogging me down.

I was mad at being sad.

For so many years, I didn't want to accept that Todd's and Scott's lives were over. I thought I could take them with me. I thought I should live for them. Do the things they never got the chance to do. But when I tried that approach, I just felt sadder. Wishing they could be with me or have the opportunity to do stuff on their own was futile. And exhausting. So exhausting. Trying to carry these 175-pound young men with me all over the place. Trying to guess what they might like to do, how they might react to a situation. I wanted to fit a life that they might have lived inside my own life. A life that I was still trying to figure out.

After years and years and years, I realized I just couldn't do it. I couldn't live the life that they missed out on. Heck, I didn't even know how to live my own life. Eventually, I concluded that I had to get over them. Pick a point in time and wipe my hands of them. Move on. Get past it.

I came up with my own version of a "Get Over It and Move On" type of grieving around the time Scott died, about seven years after my mom died.

I was tired of crying at every sad country song I heard. I was tired of missing my mom. I was tired of the heartache. Every New Year's Eve would mark the beginning and end of another year without her. Every April 23 would remind me that I missed her birthday once when she was alive and would continue missing her birthday for the rest of my life. I refused to celebrate every Mother's Day because my mom was dead.

I knew I had to get over it. It just hurt. Bad. Bad enough that I knew I couldn't carry on like this forever. But how? I had no idea how to make it go away. So I picked an amount of time worthy of my mom. Seven years. *There, that is solved.*

Not quite sure exactly when I came up with that number, but I made myself believe it. *The seven-year itch. That's a thing, right?* I had seven years to get over my mom. Likely I chose that number because I wasn't quite there yet, but it was close. That would give me some time to get rid of that pain.

Todd got two years. I had only known him briefly, after all. But the two-year period had come and gone. *Why wasn't I over him? Controlling time was going to be tougher than I thought.* But it was set in stone. Good-bye Todd, whether I was ready for it or not.

But because Mom died right after Todd, I wondered when Todd's time started. *Did I hit pause on Todd's time, then go to my mom's? Wait a sec. Did I ever even grieve my mom? How would I cross the finish line when the seven years were up if I didn't know when the seven years started?*

Then Scott died. Around that seven-year mark. *Now what!? How am I going to manage this?* I tried to answer these questions by myself, and it wasn't working.

I was still crying over my mom.

I was still crying over Scott.

And I couldn't figure out which tears were for Todd.

Then Nancy died.

It was as if I was treading water in a swimming pool, then someone threw me a balloon and told me to hold it under-water. A few minutes went by, and they tossed in another balloon. More time treading water and another balloon. More time and another balloon. Eventually, I ran out of limbs, and every single balloon rose to the surface at once. I couldn't control even one. I was out of energy, just trying to keep my nose above the surface.

I'm not sure the first time the word grieving entered my vocabulary. I know it wasn't until years after Nance died that the word grieving entered my conscience. It wasn't until after my attempt that I looked into the stages of grieving and really tried to understand it.

I realized I spent all of those years attempting to make sense of all my losses without even a first-grader's under-standing of grieving. I didn't talk to anyone about it. Really talk to anyone. I let people know I was sad, and missed those I lost, but I never really talked about it with the goal of understanding it.

I just kept plowing away at life. Get my high school degree. Go to college. Get my college degree. Get a job. Make some money. Make more money. Get a promotion. Make more money. Stay in shape. Have fun. Make more money. Go on road trips. Go visit another country. Make more money. Run a marathon. Party all weekend long. Get a new car. Go. Do. Go. Drink. Forward, forward, forward.

I gave no recognition to my feelings about losing people, losing important parts of my life. I knew something terrible had happened. I knew I was feeling different emotions, but I didn't attempt to describe them, let alone understand them. In the aftermath of any one of my losses, therapy or seeking help from a counselor wasn't emphasized. I can't recall having one discussion about dealing with loss.

I wonder if those hours I spent throwing tennis balls against the wall or miles of bike riding was my way of getting away from my parents' toxic marriage? Was that the beginning of my grieving? Or was that the beginning of the avoidance of grieving?

When Depression overwhelmed me in my thirties, I still didn't understand its relation to grief. Nor did I understand that a multitude of emotions partner with grief. Anger, sadness, peace, laughter, frustration, curiosity. I'm sure I'm forgetting some. They swirled around me. Sometimes I felt one at a time. Mostly, though, it felt like they were all ganging up on me. Then they went away. Then they came back. Their timing seemed to be impeccable.

Even after clearing alcohol from my system, so much grief still existed. A big part of my life felt like a long walk down the entirety of the Pacific Coast.

It began with miles and miles of sand, rain, and gray skies along the Washington coast with almost no visibility. Periodically there may be an inlet or bay to break up the monotony. For the most part, this portion of the coast was just an expanse of numbing openness. I just had to keep walking until I got a different view.

Then it was the Oregon coast, with its sideways rain that causes the sand to scrape the skin, intermixed with the most beautiful blue skies and green surroundings. Crashing waves pummeling the earth, with a sound that can lull me to sleep. Powerful rock formations and tall cliffs. Rivers and creeks forming inlets and bays. Beauty and the beast, how I felt about loved ones dying.

The Oregon coast evolved into the Northern California coast. A different state, but not in my mind. More splendor, more danger. The Pacific Coast is that way, contradiction after contradiction.

Eventually, I reached the surf of Southern California with its volleyball pits, bikinis and board shorts, the smell of coconut oil, and people of all ages cruising on their single-speed bikes. Though foggy on many mornings, the sun came out every day. I finally could stop walking, sit for hours, taking it all in, staring out at the ocean, and see for miles.

In my thirties, I would find myself taking this walk over and over again. Sometimes I would spend days making this walk. Other times, I would find myself at a midpoint along the journey, experiencing some kind of feeling but not really understanding why it was there.

After my attempt, with the alcohol entirely out of my being, I still found myself in a swampy mess of emotions. I couldn't describe exactly how I felt anymore. Just be able to say, "Here's the problem, I feel sad." Or angry. Or confused or silly or anything in particular at all. Since the losses had happened years prior, I could not find a specific cause or reason I could point to for having the feelings I felt. A point of reference for sharing with others. It could have been that thing that happened to me one year, or something else that happened during another year.

When tragedy strikes and one can process the grief soon after that, it can follow a process. It is overwhelming at first, but eventually that subsides and it becomes manageable. Finally, it can become a gift.

The fuzziness of me grieving multiple things at once fueled my depressed feelings. Not being able to grieve one thing at a time because they happened right on top of each other, or life just got in the way. Repeat this cycle for years, and I wound up having Depression.

Unprocessed grief seemed to build and build, like a tropical storm becoming a hurricane. For me, it resulted in developing Depression.

The counselor who ran the men's group I was a part of commented one day, something to the effect of, "We should all work toward grieving a little bit throughout all of our days."

Initially, I thought that was a weird comment. *Who wants to do that? What an awful way to live. Grieving all the time.* For me, grief was the most painful emotion I could feel. Someone died, and I had to live my life with them no longer being part of it. It fed anger, sorrow, resentment. *Why would I want more of that? Every day—was he serious?*

Even though initially it didn't make sense, I sat on that comment for a while. Loss was a big deal for me. I figured I should look at dealing with it from every angle. Maybe he had something with this regular grieving idea. If it doesn't work, it doesn't work. Because it came from Ross, there might be something to it, though.

For weeks I reflected on this. I learned to differentiate grief from the grieving process.

The simplistic version of the grieving process experts refer to are denial, anger, bargaining, depression, and finally, acceptance. Grieving the really big stuff can also include things like shock, numbness, fear, confusion, longing, helplessness, panic, frustration, testing, and hope. None of that necessarily goes in any sort of order, although most agree that the grieving process starts with denial and ends in acceptance.

Grief stinks, period, but life is full of it. I knew I needed to figure out how to deal with that. So, if there was a process out there? Sure, I'd give it a look.

Instinctively I knew working through the grieving process wouldn't be easy. But I realized that if I worked my way through it, however long and whatever nonlinear route it took, the end was well worth it. Fond memories could replace the tragic loss. Thanks could replace regret. I thought of the marathon I ran. Months of sacrifice for sure. But checking off an item on that bucket list I carry in my back pocket? Lifetime satisfaction. Maybe that is what going through the grieving process would be like.

Somehow putting a label on the phases helped, even if it didn't match the "official" tags the psych world provided. Just knowing what I was dealing with gave me a sense of relief.

With Todd's death, I went through shock and denial straight to acceptance and hope. My mom's death and then leaving Kirkland cut that grieving process short. With my mom, I stayed in pain and guilt. Scott's death just shot me straight to being bummed, then back to pain and regret over time.

I spent almost twenty years saying goodbye to my dad. Looking back, I am surprised that I feel like I handled that loss the best. It could be because I actually went through all of the phases. So much shock and denial. All sorts of pain and guilt. Angry, so damn angry. I bargained so many times, telling myself he could change, he wasn't really that bad, he could grow. Finally, I accepted that he was who he was. I had stumbled through it all. When he officially died, I was in my early forties, about thirty years after he took off, and I was able to just say, "So long, Dad."

Acknowledging the feelings and stages that make up the grieving process made the stages, which were sometimes days, or months or years, seem more acceptable.

So many times, I was lost. Just looking for my mom. Or any kind of reasoning behind the tribulation. Waiting for a nudge from someone or something that might push me in the right direction. I just wanted the medal at the end of the race, without all of the training.

What I was really looking for was acknowledgment. Like my Aunt Kay when she told me I was depressed. I needed to know that being lost, angry, or in denial was part of grieving. To know that I was grieving.

Once I felt comfortable being in that place, I could reflect. How did I get here? Am I OK being here? If so, for how long? If not, what can I do about it? Maybe run it by someone, realize that they understand, listen to their thoughts.

Of all the emotions that are part of the grieving process, anger is the strongest for me. Being mad, just mad in general like my dad was, was a darkness that I wanted no part of anymore. However, being mad because someone died seems justifiable. Acceptable. These days being angry as part of grieving some other kind of loss, anything not working out as I had hoped, also works for me. I understand it for what it is, part of the grieving process. Maybe I need to be angry before I can let it go. Or maybe the anger drives me to change something, so I achieve different results next time. At the very least, understanding that any emotion, even one as uncomfortable as anger, is just part of grieving helps me work with it rather than get frustrated at it, or deny it.

Once I understood the grieving process and that it was a necessary part of the life I envisioned living, I embraced it, used it to work through my past losses. That took time and wasn't easy or comfortable, but those steps led to my ability to work through my struggles in the present. With each journey through the process, things became easier. Struggles weren't accumulating until they became an insurmountable pile. No snowball effect.

It took me a while, but I finally understood what my counselor was talking about. A lot of little grieving was better than one big heap of massive grieving.

Grieve and go. Microgrieving. Quickly hopping through minimal steps of the grieving process for more minor life occurrences. Microgrieving being late for a meeting because of an accident that just happened might look something like this:

Am I really stuck behind this accident?

This is bullshit!

If I go up on the curb, then over the median, I might be able to get past this. Crap, I'll never pull that off.

I will never make the meeting, and I'll lose the deal.

OK, I'm going to be late. What else can I do to close the deal?

The more microgrieving I practiced, the better I was at the full-size grieving that life required from time to time. I felt like I was building resilience. Like knowing I could knock out twenty pushups easy, so if I needed to, I could get forty done. Practice doesn't make perfect. It makes progress.

I also sensed that by handling the little griefs as they crop up, I cleared out my mind and soul to better deal with the big surprises when they drop. The ups and downs and back and forth of feeling sadness, acceptance, anger, or laughing, did not proceed linearly, nor did I have complete control over when they arose. Still don't.

Each wave of emotions and realizations has its own intensity and duration. But practicing microgrieving allows me to stay buoyed during the more significant storms. I can face the emotions in a healthier way. Maybe even benefit from them.

Throughout my recovery, I used the official stages to check in with myself. Have I fully worked through a loss and come to full acceptance? If I told myself I accepted that someone was no longer part of my life, but I was never sad or in denial about it, had I really accepted it? It was vital for me to understand the answers to those types of questions.

I practiced microgrieving on the little stuff believing that, with strength built upon those experiences, I could tackle the deeper issues that might even be lying dormant.

So I checked in with myself and went through the stages. Quickly. For random occurrences, not a big deal. It was like doing multiplication tables in grade school over and over again until it was automatic. I thought that by regularly powering through this, even for seemingly mundane events, I could better manage the big grief and keep Depression at bay.

By focusing on grieving, I corralled the actions and reactions into something I could manage. I learned to acknowledge that my expectations weren't met. I didn't blame anyone, especially myself. It just happened. This is how I stayed out of the hole. It allowed me to focus on solutions instead of problems. To look forward, not backward. Most importantly for me, I was acting, not hiding.

Grieving clears my mind and soul, enabling them to find solutions. The more I could grieve and go, the more of life's chaos I could handle. If I spend a few minutes or hours or days working through the internal dialogue of the grieving stages, then my mind and soul have the energy and space to take on life again.

CHAPTER 10

Self-Esteem

I was in my mid-forties when I had a profound realization. I had virtually no self-esteem. It wasn't an easy realization. Come on, Blue Andrews could not lack self-esteem. I always thought I had self-esteem. A lot of it. More than most. I felt silly even thinking about self-esteem.

It took some prodding from my therapist and a lot of research and reflection by me. Within a couple of months, the concept made sense, in a logical Spock-from-*Star-Trek* kind of way. It took many more months for me to really feel and accept it deep down in my soul. That was a shock, and just a tremendous relief.

Self-esteem. What man even thinks about self-esteem? Isn't it innate? I thought it was in me. Heroes of movies and books seem to have unlimited self-esteem. Strength of conviction. Sean Connery. Chuck Norris. Clint Eastwood. Men. Real men. Displaying confidence.

We assume that means they have self-esteem, but do they? Being confident in what you do does not always translate into feeling good about who you are.

The worlds of sports and sales didn't allow for anything but high levels of confidence. Give me the ball, come at me, focus on me. I'm better than you are. That was the attitude you had to have. Sales managers expected swagger from their salespeople. Give me a high quota. I'll crush it. No room for wavering. You better show up every day ready to win, or you won't last long.

But here I was. I had Depression and tried to kill myself. Some shock and regret was still lingering inside of me, not staring me in the face, just hanging around. I stopped drinking, and it didn't go away. I better understood the grieving process. I accepted that life included essential pain. I knew I couldn't do it all. But something was still there, so I kept investigating this relationship between self-esteem and me.

The more I read, the more I connected with the reality that although I had done well and been confident as a salesperson, athlete, and student, that didn't translate to self-esteem. To have self-esteem required feeling inherently good about myself, that people would just like me for no reason other than just me existing. That I could be a valuable part of this world without wealth or good hand-eye coordination or a round of free drinks.

I had become so fixed on the material stuff that I couldn't see my own personality. Even when I found it from time to time, I gave it no recognition. The discovery that I didn't believe in just me was a trial in acceptance. I didn't want to believe it, but when I did, what a revelation. That was it! That was the precise, core diagnosis. After peeling back the alcohol and working through the grieving. After leaning into my support network. I had low self-esteem. That was my underlying illness.

Then, an awakening.

It felt so right. As if I knew it all along but didn't know what to call it. Or wasn't ready to accept it. Or couldn't see it through the grief and the booze.

I did now. I looked back on my life and began to recognize low self-esteem throughout.

With that admission, I finally felt I had something tangible I could focus on. Research. Discover. Explore. Reflect. I could talk and ask questions and listen. Hope replaced despair. I understood now why I was still struggling, even though I had addressed my grief and was sober. If I could believe in myself, maybe the depression wouldn't come back.

The process of finding self-esteem was the first time I'd really focused on the parts of me that no one sees. No scoreboard. No quotas. Not one person pushing me in any direction, or giving me feedback, or acknowledging anything I was doing. No need to make an impression on anyone. My primary role in my forties was that of stay-at-home dad, house husband. I was purely in a support role, partially so that I could learn to support myself.

During my formative years, teens and early twenties, I gained confidence because I was born with a particular mixture of traits and talents that led to success as measured by scoreboards. They told me what a good job I was doing.

As a kid, if an adult complimented me, I accepted it relative to something I just did, not who I was as a person. In young adulthood, positive reviews from management were about money, not me. Accomplishments and accolades. Medals, honors, cash. These were the fundamentals of my pride. External endorsement was all I knew, so I made up new scoreboards, hoping these would continue to validate me. I had confidence, even overconfidence bordering on cockiness at times, but not self-esteem.

Self-esteem is internal. It's a feeling. No clock. No score. A sense. I didn't recognize it at the time, but as my success and confidence grew, my self-esteem wasn't keeping pace.

Perhaps it was because I never had anyone tell me I was good just as I was. That I was strong, appreciated, loved for just me. I would like to believe that my mom did, but I didn't listen. Likely, I wasn't emotionally ready to hear what she was saying.

My psyche just translated any of that feedback into the context of something material. The sprout of internal affirmation didn't blossom. Grief could have clouded over it. Regardless, by the time I was a fully grown adult with responsibilities outside myself, a foundation of self-esteem didn't exist. No bedrock of self-esteem was ever laid down.

Without that internal belief in myself, I grew less and less confident with each passing year. The scoreboards became fuzzier. What was the world measuring, and how were we ranked? There was always someone better at something. Someone always had more of this thing or the other. The best football player wasn't the best mathematician. The best band couldn't build the best house. How was I going to be better than … anyone?

This was at the core of my Depression.

In my forties, after my attempt, I realized I didn't even know what self-esteem was. How could I possess it?

How could I find it now, without sports or a job, where I always sought validation? Not through glory days talk and pumping up the weekend warrior. That would continue to lead to thinking that what I did or owned would make me feel good about myself. I needed to find value within. I needed to examine the part of me that was empty.

My first step toward discovering my own self-esteem was to dive into research. If I was ever going to recognize it in myself, I needed to know what it looked like. I read books and books about self-esteem. Took self-quizzes followed by recommendations based on the results. Sometimes I felt like Stuart Smalley and his Daily Affirmations from *Saturday Night Live*. "I'm good enough, I'm smart enough ... "

I hid the self-esteem books in my office. I didn't want anyone to see that I was even contemplating this stuff, let alone researching it. Definitely didn't want my wife and kids to see it.

I kept reading, exploring other people's words and my feelings about them. Then, one day, I understood. Deep down, I didn't honestly believe that I was worth anything all on my own. Without buying anything, winning anything, or achieving anything, what value did I have? I could not come to grips with the idea that someone could like just plain old me.

When I finally realized and understood that I had only confidence, it was as if I were a blind man learning about a new procedure for gaining eyesight. I felt like my disease, the deep-rooted issue below Depression and alcoholism, had finally been diagnosed. The introspection I'd been doing since my suicide attempt had produced a root cause.

Low self-esteem.

For all of the success I'd had, for all I had accomplished, my forty years hadn't given me any belief in myself. My low self-esteem was even chipping away at my confidence, the gifts I'd been given, the things I could still accomplish. There was no belief in just me. Just Blue. No competition. No material measurements. Just me. That idea didn't occur to me until therapy and reading revealed that I severely lacked self-esteem.

I recalled the comment I made to my mom when we moved to Kirkland—that she stole my confidence. I was a self-absorbed teenager who felt righteous in his anger, so I had forgotten that her response to that statement was, "You need to think about that." Maybe now I was in a place that I could.

I learned to listen to the world rather than my own heart for opinions on who I was. I always acted based on what I thought others might want. Now I thought about being me.

The scoreboard-based confidence I once had was no longer significant. Maybe I didn't really have any confidence at all? Maybe, since what I was measuring against now had less meaning, I really hadn't been successful? Questions I needed to figure out.

I sure could argue with myself as to whether or not I was The Man. That feeling of invincibility, because I'd made it out of the poor house or overcame the loss of my mother, was now gone. I had to forget all those times I had told myself how badass I was because I wasn't my dad. How could I be much of anything after I fell so far down? I hadn't really overcome anything. I wasn't able to stop any of the demons before they wrote the nightmare stories that had been in my head.

Coming to grips with all of this was the beginning of my acceptance of myself. I couldn't keep basing my self-worth on grabbing more of the rings others set in front of me. I couldn't keep looking outward for signs of success. Trying to live up to fabricated external expectations had resulted in me on the shower floor with sliced wrists.

I also had to learn where to put limits on myself. I had to understand when to apply moderation and when to apply balance. I needed to accept that being fourth best or ninth best, or not even making the team, had no bearing on my value. Moreover, all of the drivers and indicators needed to come from within.

I struggled with those feelings, so contrary to the first forty years of my life. I just knew that what I had been doing wasn't working. In my mind, my transgression was massive enough that many changes were necessary. My habits. My mindset. My outlook.

Every day, seemingly hourly at first, I had to remind myself that external validation didn't matter. Thoughts of what other people might think would creep into my head, and I would push back. *Quit it! Let it go.*

Zero feedback comes with the territory of being a stay-at-home dad. No one praised me or gave me a medal or even let me know how cool it was that I took the time to cut the crusts off their sandwich and then made fun shapes with it. No one thanked me or gave me a bonus for picking them up from soccer, cleaning off their cleats, then washing their stinky, muddy shorts and socks.

Not that I expected a pat on the back from my very young kids or had a problem with not getting it. It did take some getting used to, though. Just doing the right thing for no reason other than I knew it was the right thing to be doing. Accepting that helped me on my journey to gaining self-esteem.

Eventually, there was a realization. Almost as if I were transported through a time machine, except the time was now. By removing the need for external validation, I was left with just me. With that came the ability to experience the freshness of the world, rather than being attached to, and basing myself on, the past.

Freeing myself of the many costumes I wore, including the one I wore at work, freed up some of the internal resources I needed to recover. The constant need to run on a hamster wheel went away and started to seem absurd. I no longer needed the gold star or the pat on the back.

While letting go of external judgment was liberating, I was presented with new problems. Accepting that those outside motivators didn't matter left me with a blank slate.

Who was I now? Who was Blue? Just Blue? What was I going to do now to find self-esteem? How was that going to happen? How long would it take? What would I be like then?

More unknowns, though at this point, I had no choice but to confront and deal with those types of questions. Putting my Depression into remission depended on it.

Now that I wasn't standing underneath a scoreboard, I decided to pull myself out of anything competitive. I knew I could never love myself if I kept looking to a scorekeeper for answers. I put my watch away when I went running. I didn't set any goals in the weight room other than to be completely exhausted when I walked out. I avoided any conversation about the possibility of a pickup hoop game or tennis at the local park. I wasn't going to compete with anyone but myself.

I knew I needed to exercise, but I really needed to learn how to exercise just to exercise. This became a metaphor for my entire view of life. I began the process of focusing my vision inward. Controlling what I could control and not worrying about others. I learned the power of being self-centered and how it actually made me less selfish.

When I was in Depression, the whole world was against me. "They" were dumb. "That" wasn't fair. Why wasn't anyone trying to help me? Everything that happened out in the world—the weather, someone dying, the stock market—was about me.

As I progressed in my recovery, some of the growth I made was in realizing that it didn't matter whether the world or others changed. I learned not to put emphasis on that. It wasn't about me. What could I do about it anyway? If I was feeling good, I would keep doing whatever it was that got me there.

Then I noticed that when I was feeling good, the world started looking good. I liked that look. I wanted more of this new view, and less of that monstrous old view. I was afraid of that old view. It was scary. I didn't even want to get two steps down the path to Depression again. What I had done was so horrific that I couldn't believe it was me who did it. It must have been someone else. Who was that guy? How could he and I even be the same person? I just wanted to do anything I could to avoid it.

Part of that meant I had to see who I was alone, without some external measuring stick to give me a sense of worth. Who was Blue without being a father, husband, friend, relative? When I switched high schools, I thought I was OK being alone. When I moved to SoCal and experienced that world, I thought I was OK being alone. After everyone died or left me, I thought I was OK being alone. But it took me just shedding everything about myself and then rediscovering what I was all about before I knew that I was OK being alone.

The vision I had was of me standing facing everyone in my life. They are a vast group that I can't see past. Acquaintances are in front of me, forming a wide line like the base of a triangle. My most important relationships—my wife, kids, family, friends that are family—they are in the very back. The point of the triangle. People with various levels of closeness to me are filling in the shape. All of these people form a triangle with a base closest to me and the point at the back.

Behind my wife, at the very top, is a mirror.

I slowly walk through the group of people, pushing my way through the triangle. As I walked past each person, it was as if I was letting each person go. I was on a journey to get to a place that was just me. I had to put everyone behind me. I went through each row of people, slowly making my way to family, then past most of them until it was just my kids and my wife. I stepped through the kids. Finally, I had to look at my wife, then push past her.

At the end of the long walk, it was just me and a mirror. I stared at myself for a long time.

Then I undressed.

I had to look at myself naked. At first, I couldn't. I stared at my feet. I quickly gazed up at my hair, barely glancing at my body. I stared at my belly button. Then my ear or my forehead, an old public presentation trick. Then back to my knees. Eventually, I took a deep breath, stared myself in the eye, and took it all in. Naked Blue.

This was me. I shook my head and took deep breaths. I kept forcing myself to stare at me. Until I came to a place of acceptance. That was me. That was all I was going to get. Nothing I could do about it, no use complaining about it. I just let the feeling linger. That's me. I was more than a body. I was Blue. And Blue was OK. I was fine just the way I was. Not perfect, but I was OK.

After reflecting, contemplating, and finally finding peace, I got dressed and slowly turned around.

It was a blank scene. Nothing but open space. Then people started to appear, as if the light of a holograph was being turned on. First, I saw Sandy. Then my kids. Then my family, and friends I considered family. Then everyone else in my life.

Eventually, everyone was there. Every single one. No one left my life because I was just me. Maybe that's what they saw all along and it was just me who needed to see me. I accepted that I didn't need them. I was just lucky to have them. I wanted and cherished them.

It was a transformative shift in the way I looked at the world, and my place in it.

Now, instead of trying to guess what others were thinking about me, I could focus on what I thought of me. I was ready to search for my true Self.

The old me was beat-up, bruised. Like finding a classic car in an old lady's barn, I was ready to take myself into the shop. Remove the dust and rust, so I could begin discovering what was under the hood. From there, I could figure out how to like myself, which, I hoped, would lead to me liking life again.

I started by questioning everything about the old me. Everything I liked was under scrutiny. Everything I didn't like, I wondered about. *Did I really enjoy something, or was my mind just playing tricks on me because I thought others might like me because of it? What activities did I enjoy? What type of people did I like being around? What was entertaining to me?* I questioned it all.

As days and months passed, new questions about me just kept coming. *Did I like Seattle? Did I like college football? Did I like chicken? Did I really like the clothes I was wearing, or had I just been hoping they would like me in them?*

Once I started to be clear on what I, just me, liked, my life became simpler. What I came back to over and over again were the things I valued the most. My health. My life. My children. My wife. That was it. Giving everything I had to those things, that made complete sense. That made me feel satisfied, content. I felt inherent goodness in what I was doing, no measuring stick involved.

My mind and soul had been freed of those conflicts of living life based on others' acceptance. Those questions about myself that I had coming out of rehab could now be addressed. I started really thinking about who I was and where I wanted to go. That opened my eyes to seeing my own value in the world.

Early in my career in the software industry, I became fascinated with the technology and the people who made it function, the engineers, programmers, developers. People like my Uncle Tom. They could punch a few keys on the keyboard, and the computer screen would jump to life. Respond to input. Create efficiencies. Answer questions. Improve processes.

I thought it was magic, and those who created it were magicians. I looked at myself as just a dumb mouthpiece whose only job was to dial a phone and set up a meeting so that the smart and important people could talk. During my entire software sales career, I longed to understand what was happening in those lines of code. Maybe even become a programmer myself one day.

I pushed the desire off because it wouldn't result in an immediate gain. I was also afraid to try, fearful of what people might think. Mainly worried that I wouldn't be able to do it.

As part of my search for me, with the freedom of knowing that it couldn't lead to anything worse than what I'd been through, I enrolled in school. Solely to learn. My second attempt at being a student became one of the biggest influences in my search for my Self.

Regardless of the outcome, just making that decision was liberating for me. I was doing something, not for the money, not for the prestige, not for anyone else. This was just me doing something for me. Friends questioned what I was doing, where this would lead. The old me would have been asking the same thing. But this was a chance to try out the new me. For the first time, I would do something just because I wanted to.

At this point in my recovery, it wasn't as if I found some kind of Zen connection with the universe and just followed my heart, '70s hippie style. The decision to go back to school was as much reactionary as anything. There was a part of me that just said: "This is not the way the old me would think. The old me tried to commit suicide. I'm not doing it the way of the old me." Nothing more complex than that.

I also hoped it would fill a deep sense of regret I'd been carrying about my first go-round in college. I was not proud of what I accomplished at the U of W. I drank my way through college and had to live with it. That sat in my craw for over two decades. Maybe going back to school would fulfill a few needs for me.

It did more than that.

My first quarter back in college was strange. Part of me felt fortunate that I was given the opportunity to cross a major item off my bucket list. The other part of me thought I was crazy to be sitting in class with a bunch of teenagers learning just to learn, with no idea what might happen if I actually liked what I was learning.

My first finals week slapped me in the face. I was cramming for tests. I was staying up late working on assignments. I was a forty-year-old man with two kids, and I was worrying about finals. *Holy crap. That is crazy. What the hell am I doing to myself?* But the big picture, learning about software development and challenging myself, felt right. Instead of complaining, I let myself enjoy that I had the resources just to explore.

After that first quarter, I settled in and just let it all unfold. I had made a decision that I felt really great about. It didn't go smoothly all the time. I doubted bits and pieces of the project the entire way. But there was plenty that made me feel good about myself. I was learning about how software was created.

Along the way, I learned about myself.

I learned that I didn't need others to make me feel good. I didn't need a sales manager or a vice president telling the company that I did a good job. I didn't need a five-figure paycheck to validate who I was. I could just feel good about making the screen turn from red to blue when clicking a button. Jumping from one page to another page when clicking on an image. Returning a column of data when inputting a few filters and hitting enter.

As long as I enjoyed it and wasn't hurting myself or anyone else, that was plenty. It took a while for that to sink in. Eventually, it did.

As I was going through my classes at Bellevue College, I would periodically check in with myself. *How did I like this? Was programming better or worse than selling? Could I do this every day for the next twenty years?* I had never asked these types of broader questions before. I had asked questions about direction and goals before, but always within a framework of money and upward mobility. Those seemed like The Big Questions at the time but now seemed less significant. I was able to ask the bigger questions now, like, "What would I like to do if I could do anything I wanted?" After all, I'd already answered the most crucial question possible. *Do I want to live?* And the answer was yes. So now the question was how?

I learned that I didn't want to go out and make a million bucks as a programmer in a big-time software company. I wasn't built for computer programming, so that likely wasn't an option anyway. It didn't feel like it was my calling. I wasn't enthusiastic about the projects that were assigned to me. I didn't feel excited when writing the code to make the computer do what the user expected. There wasn't joy in finding a bug and fixing it. Programming was interesting, but I was doing it for the learning, not the loving.

Recognizing that was slightly disheartening but also came with a sense of satisfaction. I had tried something for no reason other than curiosity and challenge and saw it through. I ended up with one-year Certificates of Achievement in both programming and database development, pieces of paper that will likely mean nothing to anyone but me. I am proud of myself for completing that.

What was most interesting about that two-and-a-half-year period was that I learned, or maybe it was a reminder, that

I loved to write. Writing was my calling. It's not that I had ever stopped writing. I loved the little bit of writing I could do in my business career. I had journaled off and on during adulthood. But the most satisfying writing I completed was during my junior high and high school journalism and English classes. I hadn't had that feeling in a long time.

This writing refresh began with me sitting in my office jotting down some lyrics to songs. Music had been a big part of my life since I was a teen, and during this time of introspection, I wanted to incorporate things I enjoyed. The problem was, I couldn't sing or play an instrument.

I shifted to poetry. Except I didn't really like reading a lot of poetry. I finally circled back to my first love—newspaper articles. I loved writing a few hundred words. Something with a clear beginning, middle, and end. I liked including a bit of research with just enough analysis. I felt good about a nice rhythm to a set of words. A pattern in the letters. A pun, a play on words. Crafting a clever passage. All of that felt so rewarding.

During computer programming school, I also found out I was OK sitting in my office for a few hours alone, just hammering away at a keyboard. I didn't need to be out meeting and greeting on sales calls. I didn't need to be in an office surrounded by people. I would be just fine if a good portion of my life was spent in solitude.

The more time I spent thinking and writing, the longer lasting the satisfaction. The structure of the piece. The back and forth ebb and flow of my thinking. The internal postulating and concluding. The weighing of ideas, prioritizing, deciding what to keep and what to throw out so that the essay felt good.

I found My Art, that which is subject only to the creator's discretion. No right or wrong. Only to do or not do. No one else needs to read it, hear it, or see it, yet I can feel good about completing it and creating my own thing. No feedback or scoreboard was needed.

I went through many iterations before realizing I wanted the writing to be more personal than a traditional newspaper article. I wanted what I wrote to better connect with readers, allowing me, in turn, to better connect with people. I didn't want to be purely objective. I wanted to reach people.

Part of stripping away the old Blue, the need for the old scoreboard, revealed that I had a strong desire to help others rather than be better than others. As I got healthier, I realized I wanted to help others get healthier. At least try. I didn't know how I would do that, but I figured I had a better chance of making that happen through my writing than through my coding.

I began with a concept for a blog about my path to wellness. That led to an idea for a book, which led to two books, this one and another, plus an actual website. That idea sat with me for months and months. I toyed around with it for a few hours here and there. Let it simmer for a while. Came back to it. Refined the idea. Questioned myself as to whether this was the next direction for me.

I concluded that it was. I had looked at code for hours and hours, trying to make sense of it, then improve it, then improve it again. How much better would it be to look at phrases and sentences and paragraphs, then try to improve upon them? Way better.

I could justify going back to school to learn computer programming because, at the very least, in this world of more and more technology permeating our lives, I would never take a step back in my career by getting more technical. Writing a book? There was no career move involved. There was no monetary substance to it. If I did happen to finish my book, that would be it. I would have a book. Doing so would take all the courage I had.

I approached my wife with the idea that the next step in my journey would be to write a book. I told her I had an idea that I really believed in. I strongly felt that it was what I was supposed to be doing next ... but would it be OK if I didn't make any money for a couple more years? That was what I was really asking.

She said I should go for it. *Whew. Thank you!*

This was another significant step in my recovery. I would embark on a project where it would be a couple of years before accomplishing something. Even then, I may or may not get one bit of recognition from sharing what I'd completed. But it felt like the right thing for me to do. Just for me. Maybe I could help someone else out along the way, but first, it was going to be all about me satisfying me.

Now that was a huge thought.

It took a belief in myself that I hadn't felt for as long as I could remember. I wondered if I ever had that amount of faith in just myself. I finally had an answer to that question about lost confidence that came up with my mom. I would find my self-confidence only after finding self-worth, after finding self-esteem.

CHAPTER 11

Wellness

After getting out of rehab and integrating myself back into life, I realized wellness would be the end goal. It had to be. Wellness was the foundation upon which I would build my new life. How—or if—I could attain it wasn't clear at first. After all, I spent twenty to thirty years of my life dealing with some level of depression. But once I stopped drinking and had worked the emotional and physical toxins out of my system, my Depression began to recede. I felt up to the task of trying to achieve wellness.

I had enough glimpses of wellness to know that was the right direction. I knew that achieving wellness would probably be the best thing for me. As I continued my recovery journey, I didn't understand what wellness truly meant, nor what it actually felt like. I wondered, *when was the last time I was actually well?*

Ideally, in today's American language, the word healthy would be interchangeable with the word wellness. Unfortunately, the common understanding of "health" felt limiting to what I was trying to achieve. Health, for most people, simply concerns one's weight. Fat or skinny. Skinny equals healthy, and fat equals unhealthy. That's what it seems most people think.

There is a business, marketing category called "Health and Wellness," as if they are two different things.

With a tiny bit of education, people may also reference blood sugar, body fat, and/or cholesterol. Many, including the primary care physicians I dealt with, consider being healthy simply not being sick. All physical.

My version of wellness needed to go beyond the physical. It also needed to include the psychological, spiritual, mental, and emotional elements of one's being. The nonphysical.

When society refers to mental, emotional, or spiritual health, there seems to be a collective eye roll. Oh, here we go. Voodoo magic. So, in general, they set it aside for lack of reality.

But being physically healthy does not equate to being holistically healthy. There are plenty of people out there with rock-hard abs and a messed-up psyche. *How can I be completely well if areas of my life are not being considered?*

When I think about my own Wellness, part of what I can do is contrast it to Depression. When I passed through depression and ended up with Depression, I felt the world was, at its core, something negative. Life was full of problems. Every once in a while, a reprieve would occur when something good happened. But that was short-lived. The difficulties just kept surfacing. Every week, every month, every year, just more obstacles. That's what life was: Obstacles. Hurdles. Hard.

Finding Wellness allowed me to start seeing life as essentially good. Every once in a while, something negative happens, or there is a bad stretch. But, when I am feeling well, they are shorter-lived and more compressed relative to the rest of my life. This is the opposite of my depressed mindset. When I feel well, I know that these hard times will be followed by goodness and good times. These days, since I better understand how to work through the grieving process, I can even find a nugget of goodness out of a period of loss.

Another aspect of wellness is feeling optimistic, the capacity to view my life as a good thing. To see my wife as the most beautiful person in the world. Finding joy in just watching my children sleeping, heads on the pillow, at peace. Having patience and understanding with anyone I come in contact with. Accepting multiple perspectives and points of view. When I am feeling well, I become better with that. I am working, at a minimum, to maintain this aspect of my life. Ideally I can improve upon it.

In general, feeling well allows me to live how I want to live— supporting others, participating fully in life. It makes me want to write a love letter to life. This incredible thing called My Life. All of it. Every emotion. All five senses. That which I can put a finger on, and that which I can't quite touch but know is there. The pieces inside me and everything around me.

Loving life. Loving me. That is being well.

My twin daughters started kindergarten during the pandemic, which meant remote learning. Whereas I went into it with a bad attitude, making up stories in my head about all the things they were missing out on, they were just excited to have their own laptops like their big brother and big sister. They loved that they got to do online school just like their big brother and big sister. They were just excited about seeing new faces on the computer screen.

Eventually, before the school year ended, my twin girls were able to go back to school. When my wife and I asked them how their first day went, they responded, "Awesome!" After some back and forth about what they did and who they saw, we shifted into planning mode for the next day, as grown-ups do. When they heard this discussion, they exclaimed, "Wait. What? We get to go back!?"

I looked at my wife and smiled. "Yes, you get to go back tomorrow, and the next day, and lots more tomorrows." The twins just giggled and joined hands, jumping up and down. They couldn't believe it. "We get to go again!"

The joy and excitement they express every single day as I walk them to school are magical. Recently, we completed our regular walk down the hill toward the elementary school and were waiting to cross the street onto the school grounds. It was all I could do to hold them back and wait for the crossing guard and her orange flag because Bobby!!! had just gotten out of his parents' car in front of the school doors. "It's Bobby!" they exclaimed. The same kid they had seen the day before, and the day before, and the day before. But there he was!

"Bobby!" they both shouted like it was The Beatles. "Bobby! Hey Bobby!" they continued to yell after we crossed the street. All I could think about was the fact that they were not supposed to be running around this part of the school. "Slow down, girls," I shouted. But a fast walk, with backpacks swinging, was the slowest they could go. I saw the smile on Bobby's face as my two daughters engulfed him with enthusiasm. Then they all held hands as they walked into school together.

Just about every day with them carries a similar level of delight. It could be blueberry pancakes. Or seeing their "best" friend, again. Or an outfit that they picked out all on their own. It takes very little to create "Best Day Ever!" Even if they said that yesterday.

For them, there is no looking back and no looking forward. It is all about right now.

The more distance between my current life and the day after my attempt, the closer I get to the way of living that my six-year-old daughters experience. Every moment is only that moment and no other moment. Each day is a new day. Each experience is unique, if for no other reason than it is a new day.

It wasn't like an understanding of wellness happened overnight or even in succession. This shift of mindset took years and is still not complete. Life can still be two steps forward and one back. But every so often, I hit a long, pleasant plateau of consecutive Best Day Ever experiences.

The idea of living in the moment is in such contrast to how I used to feel. My life consisted of a blend of what was in front of me, plus what used to be, plus what might be. I was very rarely "in the moment."

I am teased that I have an awful memory. It's true. There is so much of the life before my attempt that I can't recall. I've long wondered if that is because I never was present enough to create a memory. I was there, but I was also back in another place and over in that other place. Often, I was looking down at myself, as if from a drone, trying to determine what others might be thinking of me.

These days, there are many instances in which I want to take a photograph to capture the moment in my head, whether it is a dramatic landscape or just an everyday occurrence. I have a camera small enough to fit in my pocket with me at all times, so I could do that. It's just that I am not worried about having to take a picture of something just to remember. My mind is so much clearer these days. My thoughts can be in the moment, undisturbed. I can take mental photos and store them away. I can attach feelings to them. More signs of wellness.

Wellness has heightened my senses. My senses still need work, absolutely, but they are so much better than they were when I had Depression. Regularly I am able to see variety in my little slice of the world. Natural and manmade. Colorful and drab. Noisy and silent. It can change from day to day, from season to season. Neighbors paint their houses. Branches fall off and leaves change color. Retail signs are updated. Constant movement and flow. I see a friend's face. I see a new face. Today one bird soars overhead. Yesterday a different one pecked on the lawn I walked past.

When I'm feeling the most well, I can capture the abundant life that surrounds me.

These days, it brings me joy to hear about others' good fortune, or even just their good times. I love hearing about my friends and family taking a chance, going for it, trying something new. I like to hear their plans for the future. I am excited for them. Such a change from the cynicism I used to hold.

One of my friends, godfather to my twin daughters, lives in Ketchum, Idaho, just outside Sun Valley. The Sun Valley area is unquestionably one of the best areas of this great country, full of rivers, mountains, and pastures. Four seasons. Fall colors and spring blooms, heat in the summer, snow in the winter. Just the right amount of good food, dives, and entertainment.

There are days when my buddy can ski in the morning and fish in the afternoon. He mountain bikes, hangs by the campfire, and stays out too late when friends come to visit. He is able to make money on a schedule that is of his choosing. At a moment's notice, he will fly to Mexico or a weekend of music down South.

He is literally Living The Dream.

I would not trade my life for his.

I am happy and excited for him, not jealous. There is nothing I would forgo in my life to live in his. I am happy that he has his life, and I am overjoyed that I have mine.

I have come to realize that this is a sign of my contentment. Being content is as good a sign of my wellness as anything. To me, being content is different than being satisfied. I understand it is a bit of a gray area, but the distinction for me is important. Content is a bigger-picture feeling. Broader and deeper. Satisfaction is more short-term, goal-oriented, and about chunks of life.

I have finally reached a place of being content with who I am and my place in the world. This allows me to support others with a simple "Go for it!" or "Good for you!" on up to more significant efforts that require physical help, sustained emotional encouragement, or varying perspectives.

Being supportive also replaces being judgmental. Finding that everyday joy in what others do is part of that wellness cycle. The more I do to feel good, the easier it becomes to feel good for others, inspiring me to do it more often.

———————

Once I started to feel well again, I fell back in love with my wife. Not that I ever stopped loving her. The admiration love, the friendship love, the mother-of-my-children love, that was always there. But that type of love that happens when you first meet The One, that love that includes infatuation and lust and longing. That came back.

I love hearing her voice on the phone. I love seeing her smile and looking into her rich, blue eyes. Though we have celebrated her 29th birthday numerous times, I still think she is a hottie. I am in awe of how she manages all the aspects of her life. She moves confidently from executive to mom to daughter to friend with such fluidity and joy. So much joy, so often, becomes contagious. I can feel it radiate through our kids. Countless times I just stare at her, wondering, *how did I get to be so lucky?*

I don't believe I could have found those feelings, rekindled that level of connection, had I not been well.

When I'm really feeling well and present, I find myself with the ability to look into someone's eyes. Sometimes my self-esteem isn't where it should be, or my mind is elsewhere, and my view flits around the room like a bird's. When I can look someone in the eye and really see them, if only for a few seconds, a connection is made that buoys my being. It strengthens my resolve to continue searching for wellness.

During these moments, it feels like I can genuinely hear what they are saying, feel some level of empathy or sympathy, and better understand what they mean. I can experience the entirety of the moment, a moment that can never be reconstructed.

As I've progressed away from being controlled by Depression, I've noticed I no longer am fearful or self-conscious of others looking into my eyes. I'm OK with them seeing me. I'm OK with their interpretation of what I'm saying. I'm OK with them judging me.

When well, I can feel laughter. Not just hear it or see it. Really sense the joy coming out of someone's mouth, resonating off their shoulders, bouncing off their cheeks. Not just offer my own laugh, but join in. Combine my laughter with theirs.

I didn't forget how to laugh when I was depressed. I laughed when it was appropriate. There were slivers of joy. Feeling laughter while out from under the umbrella of Depression is different. It is like I can jump in the pool of laughter and swim around in it.

My children make me laugh almost every day. It usually happens at the dinner table, which is my favorite time as long as I am with all five others in my family. My wife and oldest kids have great senses of humor, and my youngest two still can't grasp some of the nuances of our West Coast version of the English language, so misunderstandings leading to laughter are bound to happen.

It begins with some giggling or a brief laugh, followed by laughing at the laughing, and then it's all over. I see five faces, eyes scrunched, cheeks pinched, mouths open, laughing. Laughing and laughing. Tears form in the corners of my eyes. Possibly a snort or two. I lean my head back. My eyes may even shut. I sway from side to side as I lose a bit of control while the laughter takes over.

I look around and see The Most Important People laughing, each with their own physical variances and pitches and rhythms. The laughter absorbs the food, the table, the lighting. For a few minutes, that is all that exists in the world.

I cry a lot. Call me a crybaby. I'm OK with it. I have been my entire adult life. I cried, drunk as a skunk, when I was in college, and my dad told me he wasn't going to pursue an opportunity to get his jewelry, jewelry he created with his own hands, into some regional and national chains. I cried, again drunk, at a Brooks & Dunn concert at The Gorge when a mother with her very young daughter and no adult male around reminded me of my single mom. I cried, this time sober, when I realized that I wouldn't be able to see my friend Will on a daily basis.

That was all when I was on my way down. Yet these days, working my way back up, I still cry. Somehow the crying feels better now.

I cry when I recall, the next day or the following weekend, moments of pure joy with my friends, somewhat in disbelief of my good fortune. I cry when I watch my children do something that I know is a growing moment, like achieving something in sports or the arts that they have been working so hard at. Or braving to step into an uncomfortable social situation and coming out of it with a smile. I cry when I walk away from hearing my wife be the awesome businesswoman she is. This isn't the shoulder-aching crying that happens when someone dies, but I now understand the phrase "tears of joy."

I have accepted that I am a crier. That makes it feel so good when it happens. I am an emotional person. I can't hide my emotions, even when I try. So I just let them out. Crying is a representation of the extremity of my emotions. This level of comfort doing something that is supposedly so awkward for a guy has become a sign that I am doing pretty well these days.

One gift I've been given in my recovery is that I can feel a magnitude of emotions to their extreme and quickly return to the middle. For example, I've worked out enough that I'm very comfortable getting my physical self to the point where it is dripping sweat and barely able to breathe. My muscles to the point where it is tough to turn the steering wheel. I know that my body will cool, and my breath will slow. I know that level of exertion makes me feel good in the hours and days after hitting that peak.

I look at crying, or jumping out of my seat with my hands in the air, or having my heart pound a little harder when watching my kids in action, as getting my emotional self to that point of exertion. During my life before my attempt, I wasn't always sure what was going to happen to me after peaking out during an emotional time. Before understanding how to work through the grieving process, when I was drinking to get drunk, when Depression took over my life, emotional swings had control over me. I couldn't recognize them, nor could I appreciate them. They would toss me around like a rag doll and leave me in a corner.

In finding more wellness, I have built some emotional resilience. I know that I will get back to equilibrium. I am not scared of feeling too much because I can find my way back to chill. The overexuberance or downright misery won't take over. Knowing I can bounce back allows me to fully feel emotions without fear or self-judgment.

It's not as if I am spending my days holding hands with unicorns skipping down rainbows. I am not always present and content, not always able to try my hardest, not always appreciative of the world around me and my place in it. I slip back into old habits. I have bad days or just get lazy. I know what I need to be doing to keep me feeling good, and I just don't do them.

Life still can hit hard. I lost my uncle and spent months and months angry and unable to sort out my emotions. Fourteen months later, Steve Hardie died, lumping a helping of grieving on top of the pain and confusion I was already feeling. I was not on top of my wellness for a couple of years. I wasn't feeling energetic and understanding. I couldn't really move forward, just spending my days taking care of the basics and wandering through the grieving process.

There are two things I now understand about my own wellness that stick with me, though. I know what to do to get back to being well, whether I've had a bad day or a bad few months. I also know what it feels like to be well, which I am so thankful for. To understand what it's like when everything feels right in my world. That gives me the desire to get back up, pick up the pace, and return to the process of finding my best me.

I find myself at the most peace when I walk around the house in the middle of the night, peek in on all four kids, stare at them asleep with their heads on a pillow and the covers placed just right. I just stand in the door jamb, leaning on one side, and stare. If the covers are piled too high, I will lightly creep closer to see their faces. Then I make it back to my room and crawl into my bed. Before laying my head down, I rest on an elbow, staring at my wife. I put my hand gently on her head, just for a moment, so softly as not to wake her, and smile.

My Most Important People. Safe. At this one moment, when the day is past and tomorrow is not here, they are not hurting, not worried, not anxious. They are well, and I am with them. As I drift off, I remember—life is good.

Hey Dad, life doesn't suck. In fact, it's the exact opposite of sucking. It's amazing. Why couldn't you see that?

CHAPTER 12

Recovery

The only positive thing about making it through a suicide attempt—*the only thing*—is that every day I make a conscious decision to be alive. That gives so much of my life and wellness goals a framework. If I'm going to be alive, I might as well make the best of it, be the best me I can be. Making that conscious decision to live guides the choices I make.

Before going any further, I want to be clear…Attempting suicide is not a good step to recovery, or health, or wellness. **DO NOT ATTEMPT SUICIDE.** It is an action that I have to live with for the rest of my life. There is regret that I let life get the better of me. That I didn't ask for help. That I gave up. No matter how well I've felt in the last ten years, I still feel different levels of guilt and grief on those issues from time to time.

There is the fact that I hurt my wife. She has to live with what I did as well. My kids know they have a parent who attempted suicide. How will that affect them down the line? My extended family, and friends that I consider family—how did I hurt them? That stuff sticks with me.

NO SUICIDE! Please, please, please, do whatever you can to change directions if you feel suicide might be the answer.

My life, though, does contain that decision. That night. That action. I must make the best of it, or I am destined to fall down that well again. I have realized that I am making a choice. About my life. About my Self. About my actions. They are my choice.

The first one is to be alive, which gives me the most solid foundation for growth. So basic, yet so powerful. That choice is grounding. I am making a choice today to breathe, to be a part of the world, to be a part of the lives that I encounter.

I probably know more now about how to kill myself than I should. I'm reasonably certain that if there were to be a next time, I would succeed. That's a scary thought. I can't let myself get too far down that path.

I am me, though. I stick my foot down that path of Depression from time to time. Over the past ten years, I've even felt myself take a few strides closer to it, either because life came at me hard or I lost focus. Soon I remember what's down there, lurking in the darkness at the end of that path, and I don't like it one bit. I then make all of the positive life-affirming choices I can to pull out of it.

I find a lot of similarities between Depression and alcoholism. Both are diseases I have had. Both are in suppression now. Both could be reactivated anytime if I don't make the right choices.

There are several viruses and bacteria in our body that would be negative in high quantities. Healthy immune systems suppress them, so we don't feel them and likely don't even consider them. A healthy lifestyle and a healthy attitude suppress depression and alcoholism. However, I will never forget what it's like to be consumed by them.

This is why I always consider myself living in recovery, and why I am comfortable with that understanding. I was ready to embrace any possible thing to get well. I didn't want to live any other way. What living in recovery means is repeating and refining all of those steps that brought me out of the depths of pain. Living in recovery means being able to find all of the beauty that wellness brings with it.

Much of my recovery has felt like a long hike through the red rocks and desert of the Southwest. For the longest time, I would just walk through a flatland or a valley. Not really sure which direction I was heading, looking up feeling like the sun was always right above me beating down. I was just moving forward, sometimes thirsty and exhausted. Sometimes inspired by the scenery. Ups and downs, but no big event.

Then something would cause me to make a mad scramble up a hill of rocks until I reached a plateau. Maybe something behind me, maybe something up ahead. I climbed, possibly without even considering what I was doing, until I could rest. I could look ahead at the amazing view or look back at how far I'd climbed.

Then it was more up and down, more trudging through deserts and valleys, until another painful climb to a peaceful plateau.

About five years into my recovery, I found the ability to tell myself, "Everything's going to be OK," and really believe it. It became part of a mantra for me.

Everything is fine.
I am just fine.
Everything is going to be OK.
I am going to be OK.

My mind still wants to push back. Try to convince me that I am not OK, not fine. That things aren't going to work out. I had been telling myself that for decades. However, with each year of growth, my mind pushes back less and less.

When life gets tough, I just say those four sentences to myself. To this day, it's incredible to me that I actually believe it. But I do. Moreover, I'm so thankful that I find the need to use this mantra less and less as the wellness side of the scales tips in my favor.

In recovery, and with the strength that being well brings, I remind myself that life's unpredictability is OK. That doesn't make life scary out of control. It just makes it not completely in my power. Given that, I remind myself to keep practicing recovery in all of its forms. To not forget the things that got me feeling good, refine where there are opportunities, and seek new habits as my journey progresses.

One of the most critical concepts I work on accepting is Essential Pain. Bad things that just happen as part of life. Not "traffic is terrible" bad, although even that could be a learning moment. No, Essential Pain, in my life, means the horrible stuff, such as losing a loved one before their time. I allow myself to feel the pain while also accepting that hardship is a part of life. Dealing with death. Illness. Loss. These are all parts of life. To refute this and try to deny it will only cause more pain.

My problem earlier in life had been that they always felt like bad things were happening to me rather than just happening. That followed with thinking life wasn't fair, followed by trying to blame something, and ended without answers and a whole lot of anger. Not having answers for the big stuff led to not having answers for the little things in life that are sure to happen. So I struggled with accepting change, any kind of change, because I didn't want to bother with grieving over things out of my control. I wanted to hold onto the past while grabbing for the future.

It took multiple discussions with my therapist about this Essential Pain for it to finally stick. I didn't understand it at first. Seemed like a bullshit psychobabble concept. *But what if I don't want pain. Why does pain have to exist? Why should any pain be "essential"? Shouldn't the goal be pure happiness?*

When my Depression was at its deepest, the unanswerable question became, *When is the pain going to stop?*

But the more I heard about the term, Essential Pain, and the more I discussed what it was all about, the more fascinating it became. After all, fighting against life didn't do me any good. Might as well figure out how to work with it.

These days there is no shoulda, coulda, woulda about pain. People die. Bodies change. Chapters conclude. All of this happens whether I like it or not. But I do grow from it. At the very least, I learn what it's like, so I can pass on that information to my kids or others who have yet to experience it. At its best, Essential Pain gives me new insight into life. It provides a fresh perspective that leads to a better understanding of the world and the people around me.

While I don't welcome Essential Pain, I do appreciate it.

Recovery is a process, and life repeatedly throws unexpected curveballs, curveballs that are tough to hit.

I don't live in fear of this. I just acknowledge that recovery takes effort. At times, I may need to increase or hone my skills, which includes reaching out to my support network or going through the grieving process. But the key is to acknowledge life's snags and make an effort. "What's the most important thing?" I ask my kids. By now, all four can answer in unison, "Trying." When we are growing up, that can answer just about all our development and struggles. Just try. For adults, there tends to be more emphasis on succeeding than on trying. Even so, over ten years into my recovery, I find "trying" to be a pretty good answer to many of life's situations.

Any type of growth that I've had in recovery has required trial and error. The idea of trying ten things to find only three or four that work used to be frustrating and seemed like a waste of time. Now, I can think of that as a success. And with practice and luck, maybe the next time, it will only take me five tries to find a couple of things that work. I find comfort in knowing that, even if something doesn't serve me, it is better to have tried than to look back and wonder if I should have gone for it.

I have learned to get satisfaction from just trying. I don't need points on the scoreboard. I just need to get on the field. The difference between being well and sick, in this regard, is that I'm comfortable not knowing the outcome. I'm comfortable failing. Trying has become more important than succeeding. As long as I'm trying, I'm not going back down the dark path.

So many "tough guys" I know scoff at the idea of participation awards. But, in a long life, that's really all there is. Doing. Going for it. It's not specifically about one thing or another. It is more about me just doing something in a positive direction. Instead of just living with sadness or anger, I am doing something to counter it. That's what has been a keystone to my recovery.

Sometimes I've made the wrong decision. I couldn't quite pull off making my own kefir or do gluten-free bread. Found out CrossFit wasn't for me. Realized nightly reflection just caused my mind to take off, impairing my sleep. As much as I respect him and recommend people open up one of his books, Eckhart Tolle just isn't for me.

That wasn't and isn't the point. What made me feel good, and, thus, what kept me working in a positive direction, was that I was trying healthy things.

Just as the cycle of being sad, not grieving, not exercising, then getting sadder was a cycle, this process of finding my healthy living lifestyle has been a cycle of improving in one aspect of my life so that I can improve in another area, which then helps me with the original part. Try something, feel better, try some more. It will continue to morph as I age, my body ages, the requirements of my environment change.

I have changed the serenity prayer to a serenity mantra. A prayer feels passive, more of a wish. I find that when I take action, I feel better.

> *Seek* *serenity so I can accept the things I cannot change.*
> *Seek* *courage so I can change the things I can.*
> *Seek* *wisdom so I will know the difference.*

It is not a question. It is a statement, a command.

One of the areas I still struggle with is eating for the wrong reasons. It's probably better than drinking for the wrong reasons, but still not healthy. At times I eat out of emotional distress or boredom instead of eating for sustenance and growth. If the world isn't going exactly as I had planned in my head, I will tackle a box of ice cream. If enough minor frustrations pile up that I become cynical at the world once again, I will devour foods that I know will make me feel bad.

Early in my recovery, I did this frequently. Purposefully hurting myself. Actions like these were part of my mental instability before my attempt, so I didn't care back then. Now I was working toward wellness, so it bothered me. For some reason, I couldn't stop. I couldn't summon enough motivation to make a beneficial, rather than destructive, choice. Eventually, though, I became angry enough that I tried something different. I had an incentive to change bad habits.

In this sense, anger was a good thing.

Anger is not normally an emotion that we associate with a positive outcome. In this case, though, it was. It drove me to change my actions for the better. Accepting a "bad" emotion as something good cemented a concept I'd learned from my therapist. Emotions can't categorically be put in a good or bad pile. Emotions just are. They just exist, as do trees, dirt, and people different from me. Arguing that some emotion shouldn't be there or doesn't exist is like trying to knock out water.

Once I became comfortable with that concept, working with a challenging, big emotion became much easier than fighting it. It became much easier to accept my emotions rather than judge myself for having them.

Over time, I began to see that many so-called "negative" emotions could serve a purpose. I would allow them in, although sometimes reluctantly, and use them. Sadness often brought me to tears, which released some pain or helped me through the grieving process.

Is sadness "bad" in this scenario? Is joy a "good" feeling if it is causing someone else pain?

Emotions, like people, are complex. They do not fall into binary good or bad buckets. In my recovery, I learned that I needed to see them, recognize them, become curious about them, and accept them as part of my Self. Improving my self-esteem was a significant factor in being able to do this.

Upon accepting that emotions are, I found myself better able to give a proper name to whatever I was feeling. That lessened it in my mind. Which resulted in me dealing with it better. I became less emotional through this practice and more able to work with how others felt. I could hear my kids and others who are close to me because I wasn't trying to figure out what was happening inside me.

Not being able to recognize or make sense of an emotion can complicate a situation. New emotions such as frustration or confusion add to our existing internal emotional stew. Denying a feeling is usually worse. It is a battle that can't be won because if I don't accept an emotion today, I will be forced to accept some mangled, more potent form of it in the future.

An emotion is just an emotion. What matters first is that I accept any feeling that enters my mind. Secondly, what matters is what I do with that emotion. How is this emotion serving, or not serving, me? What is its purpose? How can I make use of it? Using such questions was monumental in my recovery.

Being grateful for the small stuff has also been essential to my recovery. That's what requires the most work and provides the most reward. Reeling in a big fish out in tropical waters or looking at that big bonus check, that kind of stuff is easy. It's celebrating the toast that didn't get burnt, or the child that makes it through a meal without spilling, that I find important. If I have a day where I can pause, just for a second or two, and appreciate those sorts of things, then I know I'm taking the proper steps in my recovery.

Gratitude is an excellent barometer for wellness. I continually check in with myself and ask if I'm thankful. Bonus points if I'm able to verbalize my gratitude.

It may feel like a Hallmark afternoon special to say that being grateful matters, to remind oneself to seek gratitude. Thankful for this. Grateful for that. But I have learned that I just can't survive if I'm constantly lamenting the downsides of life. I absolutely must find the positive and then recognize it with some gratitude.

The more I looked for things to be thankful for, the more I forced myself to say thanks, the easier it became. It no longer felt like some forced daily affirmation. It just became natural. One of my favorite sayings in all music was written by Billy Joe Shaver. It's the last couple of lines to his song "Mother Blues."

"And the days that I keep my gratitude higher than my expectations, well, I have really good days."

Gratitude begets gratitude. If I can be thankful for that little thing, then I can be thankful for something else. When the really good stuff comes along, I can fully appreciate it, and it sticks with me longer.

Being grateful helps me be present. Rather than focusing on what is next or what has already happened, soak in where I am and who I am with.

Wherever you are, be there.

No matter how much I love and believe in that saying, I still constantly need to remind myself of it. When I've decided to do something, be with certain people, at a certain place, for a certain time, and my mind starts wandering, I remind myself to *Be Here*. I even bought a watch with the word **NOW** written on the face in big, bold letters.

What time is it? Now.

Mindfulness is a trendy term these days. The media has associated it with meditation. Mindful meditation. Mindfulness is critical in getting your brain to a state of meditation. However, that reference takes it too far for me. Just being mindful is tough enough and gives me plenty of purpose. I personally separate the word meditation out as its own activity.

Mindful. Aware of the situation, recognizing what is happening right here, right now. Being present goes beyond just forgetting about the past and not worrying about the future. That still creates too large of a time window. That can keep me focused on yesterday, today, and tomorrow. But to get the real benefits of being present, I work to narrow down my thinking to these few minutes. That's it.

Being able to be present results in recognizing emotions and feeling gratitude. They are intertwined.

Life slowed down for me when I started thinking about now—today, the next few hours. It was a similar, but more powerful, effect as when the rehab center took care of my food, schedule, and sleep so I could focus on recovery.

Removing as much of the past and future as possible from my daily living freed up my mind to take in what was happening. Not what might happen. Not what could have happened. But what was actually happening. It sounds so obvious now. Not easy, just obvious. Back then, a few years into my recovery, it was a revelation. My entire life had been about *not* focusing on now, which resulted in regret and anxiety.

I found strength in being present because I discovered life was pretty good right now.

I never had perfect predictions about the future. I sure could poke holes in my past. But right now? Just right now? Things were usually OK. That led to the next moment being OK. Then the next. Until I'd strung together a whole day of OK-ness. Then a week. Eventually staying present led to being fine. That opened the door to times that were way better than just fine.

Being present entails being self-centered. Not selfish. Self-centered. While the definitions of self-centered and selfish are close, I make sure to remind myself of their differences. Acting selfishly is something I try to avoid. However, the first definition of self-centered in Merriam-Webster is "independent of outside force or influence." That version is so huge for me, given my history of looking outward to find my own value.

For example, this is what being selfish felt like to me.

I used to push every corner of my life. Working hard and playing hard was just a start. I thought I was invincible. I wanted extremes. In recovery, I realized that much of that drive to push everything to the limit was about external rewards, the scoreboard, the promotion, the nice car. I pushed the bounds of my capabilities because I was always looking outward for a sense of value.

I was also acting selfishly, partially because I didn't know better, but partly because I could. When I was single, I could be hungover, short-tempered, and stressed because the only person I was hurting was myself. Add in a wife and four kids, plus other things such as houses, extended family, and retirement, and my misguided drive—a symptom of my selfishness—negatively affected others and became a burden on me.

Looking back, I now have a better understanding of selfishness. It's why I can distinguish between being selfish and self-centered.

As part of being self-centered, one of the things I try to do these days is undercommit. Just in case life happens, and it usually does.

I know that I need to leave some buffer between me and the maximum. There has to be room for error, or the unpredictable, the unexpected. If I decide that pushing the envelope is what I want to do in the short term, I build in some time on the back end for recovery. I leave the calendar open one day a week. Or a weekend a month.

I feel more comfortable when there are some empty spaces. I am more relaxed emotionally and mentally. I am more rested physically. I don't feel rushed. I am less forgetful. I have some patience to give. This acknowledgment of what my Self needs, and giving it to me, is an aspect of being self-centered that I find valuable.

The second word in that phrase has become a powerful one for me. Centered. Being in equilibrium is crucial to recovery. Not too full, not too hungry. Not too much sleep, not too little sleep. Not exuberant, not sad. Not alone, not overcrowded. Goldilocks living.

Our bodies like to find homeostasis—feeling just the right temperature, absorbing just the right nutrients, taking on just the right workload. Emotionally, we are at our best when contributing but not overburdened. Some stress is good. Too much is bad. Love is good. Stalking is bad.

Balance. The center of the fulcrum.

Beyond my own wellness, one of the reasons I commit to being self-centered is because I have a core belief that healthy, well people naturally want to connect and serve. We are built for it and thrive on it when we can find it.

The better I feel about myself, the easier it is to be a better parent. A better husband. A better friend. I can listen better. I can ask better questions. I feel more open to new ideas, maybe because I'm not so bogged down trying to figure out my own. It is hard to help someone move a new bed into their house if you have a bad back or bad knees. It is hard to support someone working through the loss of a loved one if you are troubled about your own existence. It is hard to be a patient and understanding parent if you are tired and anxious.

Thus, I work to be well and balanced. Healthy physically and nonphysically. I spend extra time making sure that I am as close to 100% as possible so that when life presents me with an opportunity to help someone out, I am able.

One of my favorite parts of recovery is connecting with others in recovery. I find such inspiration in this action.

The people I have most enjoyed spending time with are others who are forward-looking also. Of course, anyone in recovery must spend some time looking back. It is impossible not to regularly reflect and expect to find wellness.

I have found that once a person finally realizes how great life can be without drugs and suffering from emotional and mental issues, they accept this lifestyle called recovery. Those are the ones who fortify me.

I gravitate toward people who are trying to improve themselves. Searching for ways to be a better version of themselves. They are the people who inspire me. They are the ones who I seek out regularly.

I like to go on walk-'n'-talks with people I can relate to. Women seem to be really good at this. Men, not so much. Men don't like to talk about their feelings. The walking part, though, is equally as hard. Men don't look at walking as doing something, as exercise. Actually, they don't really consider walking at all. Unless it's chasing a little white ball down a very long lawn.

I love walking and talking. Versus sitting and talking. Or moving and not talking. Or, what many men do around sporting events, silent sitting. For me, the combination of moving my body while fleshing out ideas about living is tremendously effective. It offers exercise, reflection, and connection all in one activity.

In the later part of my recovery, the last couple of years, I've worked on sharing my vulnerabilities. For me, it's an essential part of both connecting with and recognizing my emotions. The most challenging involves being sad, lost, or scared. My initial reaction to sharing that sort of thing is, "They don't want to hear that from me," or "They won't really care," or "I don't want to burden them with this, don't want to bring them down."

However, my well-being takes a hit by accepting those assumptions, and I miss out on possible growth. Sometimes, to get perspective and advice, I need to get an issue out from behind my eyes and in the view of a supporter. Maybe it really is a big deal, and it requires action. Or, perhaps, as you talk about it with someone else, you realize that this thing you're dealing with just needs more time. Most often, it ends up not such a big deal after all.

I also find that sharing my own vulnerabilities allows others to open up with their own. They can go through the same discoveries I do. They may have just needed prompting.

The coolest thing that happens when I share my own feelings is when it leads to aiding someone outside my network, a friend of a friend. When I can share an issue or obstacle I'm working through, and it leads to a connection with others who feel the same way, or went through the same thing, it bolsters my mindset. I am reminded that I am not alone in going through a situation or thinking from a particular perspective.

That's the minimum benefit. If it begins a dialogue or gives me the courage to continue when I'm not sure, then I've grown. If what I share helps another grow, it helps fortify my wellness journey. I don't always see the fruits of my labor clearly. But when what I'm doing to help my growth results in someone else's growth, bam, that's the vision.

A corollary to sharing vulnerabilities is sharing the stuff that makes me feel good. Letting people know not only that I'm feeling good, but what I'm feeling good about. What I did that brightened my day. Something that I'm proud of. The hope is that I could be an example of how they could look at their life. This also continues to be a challenge for me.

It took reaching a certain level of self-esteem for me to share that which exposes my authentic Self. Because the response almost always isn't what I expected, and many times it isn't good. Maybe the person I want to share something with just isn't ready for it. They may be in a bad place themselves or just don't have time. But my self-esteem is strong enough now that I didn't take that as an insult. Being OK with being vulnerable results from feeling comfortable with myself, knowing that I can take the bad with the good.

Recovery isn't always easy, and very seldom is it straightforward. Sometimes there's the little tap, tap, tap on the shoulder of my life before recovery. The stupidity of my drinking or the selfishness of my Depression. Sometimes it's a loud, bullhorn-announced reminder of my attempted suicide.

These days, I read about the number of "deaths of despair" (suicide, drug/alcohol overdose, and alcoholic liver disease) and think about what I did. People casually mention having Depression or feeling depressed, and I think about how I was acting. People refer to a friend or a family member who lost everything because of drugs, and I think about what I did.

Sometimes the topic of suicide comes up, and people will say, "How can they get that way? I just can't imagine." *Well, I know. I can imagine!* But I can't discuss it in everyday social settings. "I tried to kill myself once" isn't really something you bring up between the chips and seven-layer dip. So I remain burdened during my journey, though the load becomes lighter with every passing year.

The bullhorn announcements keep me on my toes.

I was with my wife walking through a mall one night when we passed by a knife store. We needed a couple of new knives for the kitchen, so we popped in. No one else was in the shop, so the lady behind the counter immediately chatted us up. "Looking for anything in particular? What do you need to cut?" She started handing me a couple of different options. "Get the feel of it in your hand," she said. "Notice the different blades and handles."

Very quickly, my wife said we needed to go. She rushed out of the store without me. I paused, considered, and told the lady thank you. I caught up with my wife a few doors down. She said that watching me hold the blade alarmed her. It brought back memories of that fateful night.

It had been seven years since my attempt.

I have two scars on my right wrist and one scar on my left wrist, the results of the fourteen stitches required to sew me up after I tried to kill myself. They remind me that I've come a long way, but I need to keep evolving to avoid more scars.

Recovery and all it entails—emotionally and physically, the struggles and growth, rising and falling and twisting—is an ongoing process. Formally declaring *I want to live* is my personal singularity, the point in which everything after that moment is different. That moment in the shower with the razor blade was big, one of the biggest things I've done in my life. But the most profound and far-reaching decision of my life is the one that I make every day.

I choose life. To live life. Fully live life. Not just be alive but explore and experience and feel life.

I then constantly ask myself The Two Big Questions:

What life do I want to lead?

What type of person do I want to be?

Jumping from just "I want to live" to "I want to be" and "I want to act" is a supersized leap in terms of thought, effort, view. It took some time for me to figure it out, and I am constantly observing, questioning, reflecting, and revising. The details change over time, but that is the essence of my recovery. I try to focus energy toward living, getting whatever extra days I can squeeze out of my time, and maximizing them while I have them. Any energy spent in the other direction sucks resources away from that.

By choosing to live life, I am choosing to live in recovery. That choice has given me this beautiful, awesome life I have.

Acknowledgments

I have attended exactly one writing conference, and in that conference exactly one workshop. It was led by Bill Kenower. He became my writing coach. I am so grateful that our paths crossed and that he continues to support me and my writing. I could not have written this memoir without his input and direction.

Bill introduced me to Corbin Lewars, my amazing editor and awesome cheerleader. I am so thankful for her guidance and motivation.

Thank you to Luminare Press, just an outstanding organization. Everyone I worked with has been great. I hope to be able to thank each one of them in person someday.

Thank you to all of my friends who read versions of this book and provided feedback. Rob, Kath, Cristofer, Lori, Seth, Baylor, Brad, Steve, JT, Chris, John, and Erin—thank you so much for your time, your thoughts, and your caring. I appreciate you probably more than you know.

A special thanks to Stephen, who gave me the final push I needed to complete this book.

The biggest thanks goes to my wife, Sandy. She is the most incredible person I know. She kept the house, our family, and her career in order while I fell down and began getting back up. I also want to thank those of you who supported her during that time. You know who you are.

I don't think it's overstating things to say that Sandy saved my life. She gave me what I needed so that I could find my way. I am not exactly sure how to properly say thank you for that, but I figure the best way is to continue working on being the best me possible.

Made in the USA
Las Vegas, NV
01 September 2022

54524496R00135